JOHN STUART MILL
on Ireland

JOHN STUART MILL
on Ireland

with an essay by Richard Ned Lebow

ISHI

A Publication of the
Institute for the Study of Human Issues
Philadelphia

62033

Manufactured in the United States of America

Library of Congress Cataloging in Publication Data:

Mill, John Stuart, 1806–1873.
    John Stuart Mill on Ireland.

    Includes bibliographical references.
    CONTENTS: Lebow, R. N. J. S. Mill and the Irish land question.—
Mill, J. S. Editorials from the Morning Chronicle.—Mill, J. S. England
and Ireland.
    1. Irish question—Addresses, essays, lectures. 2. Land tenure—Ire-
land—Addresses, essays, lectures. I. Lebow, Richard Ned. J. S. Mill
and the Irish land question. 1979. II. Title.
DA950.M47   1979   941.508   78–13054
ISBN 0–915980–46–0

For information, write:

Director of Publications
ISHI
3401 Science Center
Philadelphia, Pennsylvania 19104
U.S.A.

CONTENTS

J. S. MILL
and the
IRISH LAND
QUESTION

Richard Ned Lebow

THE CLASH between society's interest and the rights of the individual was a central problem in nineteenth-century Britain. It was at the root of the struggle over suppression of the slave trade, over factory legislation and Irish reform. The Irish case was unique in both the extent of state intervention desired by some proponents of reform and their willingness to tamper with property rights which most Victorians viewed as the very foundation of civilized society.

Victorians were sincerely committed to alleviating the worst social ills of their society. Chief among these was the festering sore of Ireland, a land whose inhabitants lived in penury and periodically resorted to violence in opposition to British rule. There was a consensus in Britain that the ills of Ireland could ultimately be traced to an unproductive and inefficient agriculture. Here agreement ended. English economists, depending on their view of property rights, advanced two very different conceptions of how the transformation of Irish agriculture was to be achieved. The first conception, rooted in the orthodox view of property rights, favored the development of a capitalist system of agriculture as the means of bringing prosperity to Ireland. Defenders of a second view, which took as its objective the security and welfare of the local inhabitants, advocated parliamentary action to improve the status of tenants, thereby giving them greater incentive to upgrade their methods of farming.[1]

Those who held the traditional conception, including

all the classical economists, viewed with alarm the sub-division of Irish estates brought about by the burgeoning population in the pre-famine years. Representatives of this school of thought included David Ricardo, Nassau Senior and Robert Lowe.[2] They opposed small holdings, increasingly prevalent in Ireland, as inefficient and un-economical and believed that subdivision only encour-aged population growth. They looked toward land clear-ances and emigration as effective means of coping with surplus population and of facilitating the development of large, efficiently run farms.[3]

Critics of this view, of which there were a growing number, were disturbed by the social dislocation asso-ciated with the development of capitalist agriculture in Ireland. In their opinion, clearances, the consolidation of estates and the change from tillage to grazing, all mani-festations of capitalist development, were responsible for widespread discontent among the peasantry.[4] Clearances were described as particularly cruel because the com-mercial and industrial development of Ireland was insuf-ficient to absorb the population expelled from the land. Evicted peasants faced the choice of emigration, assum-ing they possessed sufficient funds to pay their passage, or of competing with other peasants for the diminishing amount of rentable land. Such competition, a govern-ment commission found, drove up rents, making the peasant's profit margin increasingly meager and even nonexistent in bad years.[5] While the famine (1845–49) eased this pressure to a considerable extent by depleting the population, British policy during and after the fam-ine only exacerbated the dissatisfaction of the Irish peas-antry. Agrarian violence, directed against landlords and their agents, remained a chronic problem.[6]

According to the critics, the solution to the Irish prob-lem lay in transforming the rural population into peas-ant proprietors, a mode of agriculture thought to be in harmony with both the wishes of the peasantry and the character of the Irish countryside. They defended peasant proprietorship as economically feasible, citing the examples of Belgium, Switzerland and Prussia where small holdings had been made profitable. Peasant proprietorship was envisaged as a long-term goal. In the interim, the government was called upon to introduce legislation that would provide some security of tenure, establish fair rents and compensate tenants for the value of improvements they made on the land. These measures were seen as absolutely essential if the Irish cultivator was to be given a durable and certain interest in the results of his labor. Without such an interest on the part of the tenants, no agricultural improvement could be expected. The most articulate spokesmen for this point of view were Sharman Crawford, Poulette Scrope, Gavan Duffy and Isaac Butt.[7] Abroad, it received the support of Friedrich von Raumer and Gustave de Beaumont.[8]

John Stuart Mill's thought about the Irish land question incorporated aspects of both views and offers insight into how intelligent Victorians coped with the apparent contradiction between the requirements of domestic tranquility and the rights of property. Mill's interest in Irish matters went back at least as far as the debate over Catholic Emancipation, finally enacted in 1829.[9] In the 1830s he took an active interest in the question of whether or not some kind of Poor Law should be introduced in Ireland and carefully read the existing literature on the land question.[10] Mill's first major statement on that subject appeared in his *Principles of Political Economy,* first published in 1848 and almost immediately recognized as a seminal work.[11]

In this work Mill advanced a revolutionary theory of property. The old school of political economists had made the assumption that private ownership of property was basic to economic relations. Mill rejected the legitimacy of absolute property in land. He argued that land, a vital commodity, limited in quantity and not produced by man, was part of the common heritage. Property rights were therefore "subordinate to the general policy of the state" and the only absolute right of landowners was to fair compensation in the event of being dispossessed by the state.[12] It should be pointed out that this argument was a theoretical one and not envisaged by Mill as the justification for any program of action. He advocated no changes in the laws of tenure and landholding in Britain nor any large-scale state action to redistribute property. Rather, Mill perceived a definite social advantage in supporting the custom of property rights because it encouraged landlords to make improvements for themselves and their posterity.[13]

In England property rights and capitalist agriculture were effective institutions, Mill believed, because of the enlightened character of most landlords and the diligence of their tenants. This was not the case in Ireland. In the *Principles* he repeatedly castigated Irish landlords as profligate absentees interested only in squeezing the last penny from their land. The existence of a parasitic landowning class together with the large number of people already residing on the land made the introduction of capitalist farming "wholly impracticable." "The people are there," he argued, "and the problem is not how to improve the country but how it can be improved for its present inhabitants."[14] Following the lead of Crawford, Scrope and others, Mill saw the solution in the gradual introduction of peasant proprietorship. This was to be achieved by redeeming large estates, reclaiming wastelands and distributing the land among the peasantry. Mill was adamant in his defense of the feasibility of peasant proprietorship and devoted two chapters of the *Principles* to the subject.

For Mill, security was the fundamental condition of prosperity because it gave the farmer an interest in increasing the value of his property. A lack of security was responsible for the ills of the Irish countryside. Improving tenants were as often as not evicted or charged more rent. The interest of the tenant was therefore inimical to agricultural development for it consisted of running down the land in the hope of extracting what profit he could before his short lease expired. Mill was fond of quoting Arthur Young on this point: "Give a man the secure possession of a bleak rock, and he will turn it into a garden: give him a nine years' lease of a garden, and he will convert it into a desert. The magic of property turns sand to gold."[15]

Since Irish landlords were too shortsighted to grant a reasonable degree of security to their tenants, it became necessary for the government to intervene. Mill accordingly spoke in favor of introducing some kind of fixity of tenure and of compensating tenants for improvements. He thus appeared to be a wholehearted supporter of the critics of classical economics and the *Principles* was frequently cited by proponents of peasant proprietorship as providing a theoretical underpinning for their position.[16]

Mill's prescription for Ireland was a logical extension of his theoretical analysis of the nature of property and the causes of agricultural prosperity. However, Mill the practical man and libertarian drew back from the radical conclusions of Mill the political economist. The introduction of peasant proprietorship was in essence a call for the total restructuring of the Irish economy by the state. That Mill found such a prospect terrifying is made apparent by the disclaimers he included elsewhere in the *Principles*. In the original edition as well as in the five revised editions which appeared up through 1865, he inserted passages mitigating his criticisms of Irish landlords and, in the revisions, he actually retracted his endorsement of fixity of tenure.[17] The worst kind of landlord, he declared, was in fact in the minority.[18] Fixity of tenure, the linchpin of peasant proprietorship, he began to oppose for the same reasons advanced by more orthodox economists. It would constitute, in effect, the wholesale expropriation of the Irish aristocracy, a measure that might have incalculable political repercussions. It would also discourage or even prevent the development of large productive estates by entrepreneurs with capital to invest. Mill even suggested that there were many such landlords in Ireland despite the fact that the famine had left the Irish propertied classes nearly destitute. At other points in the revised *Principles,* he expressed concern that under a system of peasant proprietorship estates would be divided into very small units, farms too small to be profitable. He also questioned the moral character of some of the peasantry, who were not the kind of persons one would want to trust with property.[19] Mill ended up ruling out state interference with the rights of landlords with the exception of legislation aimed at reclaiming wastelands.[20]

These notions were so contradictory to the empirical arguments Mill had laboriously developed elsewhere in the *Principles* that they lacked credibility. Further evidence that Mill was desperately trying to find some means of creating a prosperous, secure Ireland without massive state intervention can be adduced from his scheme to reclaim wastelands. The suggestion that the state should settle surplus population on reclaimed land was first made by W. T. Thornton in 1846.[21] Mill fixed upon the idea at the height of the famine as a possible solution to his dilemma. He became so absorbed with the scheme—perhaps another indicator of the psychological function it served—that he halted work on the *Principles* to devote himself entirely to its propagation. Between October 5, 1846, and January 7, 1847, Mill exploited his free access to the editorial page of the *Morning Chronicle* to contribute forty-three unsigned articles on Irish affairs, the majority of them in support of reclaiming wastelands.[22] In these articles, the gist of which was subsequently incorporated in the *Principles,* Mill advocated settling 1.5 million peasants on as many acres in western Ireland. He acknowledged that this might require compulsion but justified that in terms of the results that would be produced. Such a population transfer together with "very moderate" emigration would remove enough people from land already under cultivation to facilitate "the introduction of English capital and farming" over the greater part of Ireland.[23]

This neat solution to the Irish agricultural problem held out the promise of reconciling the interests of the peasantry with the rational economic development of Ireland, objectives which other economists had found to be laudable but incompatible. The critics, of whom Nassau Senior was the foremost, hastened to point this out.[24] They were right. Not only did the scheme have little chance for adoption, it was unrealistic in the extreme.[25] The element of compulsion aside, the west of Ireland, where Mill hoped to settle 1.5 million peasants, consisted largely of barren and unproductive land. It was hard to imagine how even with the most intensive farming methods it could support half that number. Moreover, the results of previous attempts at reclamation, with which Mill was undoubtedly familiar, were very discouraging.[26]

The prospects for peasant proprietorship appeared to diminish throughout the 1850s and early 1860s. Ireland was tranquil again and over-optimistic parliamentarians even spoke of agrarian violence in the past tense. Beyond this, economists exaggerated the changes wrought by the famine, especially the extent to which it had cleared Ireland of small farmers. *The Times* predicted that "a Celtic Irishman will be as rare in Connemara as is the Red Indian on the shores of Manhattan."[27] This prophecy of rapid rural progress ignored the fact that the Irish landowning class, which had been made to absorb the cost of famine relief, had been left without capital to modernize its estates. Improvements in the post-famine agricultural situation, largely the result of price changes which accelerated the transition from tillage to grazing, nevertheless made it appear that no radical measures were required. Parliament, in any case, was not about to support any bill that tampered with the property rights of landlords.[28]

Even Mill was infected by this optimism. In the editions of the *Principles* which appeared in 1862 and 1865, besides arguing that fixity of tenure was no longer needed, he favored rooting out the remaining small tenants in order to facilitate effective consolidation of Irish estates. Mill saw the continuing existence of the Church of Ireland as the established church to be the last justified grievance of the Irish people.[29] He even compared the Irish to the Bretons to justify and explain their political assimilation to Britain:

> When the nationality which succeeds in overpowering the other is both the more numerous and the most improved; and especially if the subdued nationality is small, and has no hope of reasserting its independence; then if . . . governed with tolerable justice . . . the smaller nationality is gradually reconciled to its position, and becomes amalgamated with the larger.[30]

The complacency of the economists was shattered by the Fenian rebellion. Organized in 1858, the Fenian Brotherhood was dedicated to overthrowing the British yoke by violent means; its leaders believed that nothing could be accomplished through constitutional forms of redress. Fenianism thrived on widespread agrarian discontent but offered no program of social action other than national independence. Although the Fenian insurrection in March 1867 was a tawdry affair that collapsed in a single night, its failure did not lead to a surcease of violence. It spread to England where rebellion was supported by large numbers of Irishmen who had earlier fled there to escape from the famine. In September 1867, for example, Fenians killed a policeman while freeing two activists from a Manchester prison. In December, they killed twenty people in a bomb explosion at Clerkenwell.[31]

The Fenian attacks touched off a wave of anti-Irish fury. They also led more thoughtful Englishmen to ponder the nature of and remedy for the dissatisfaction in

Ireland that underlay both the violence and demands for independence. J. C. Beckett observes that "It is an error to suppose that it was Fenianism that first turned Gladstone's mind to Ireland; but it was Fenianism that disposed the British public to accept the remedial measures that he was shortly to put forward."[32]

The first important statement linking Fenianism to the land tenure question was made by Isaac Butt in his pamphlet *Land Tenure in Ireland: A Plea for the Celtic Race,* published in July 1866.[33] Having defended Fenian prisoners Butt could claim to speak with some authority about the nature of their grievances. He argued that the Irish people had never accepted the alien system of landed property thrust upon them by the English and that their discontent had actually increased in the postfamine years. This was so because the last vestiges of their traditional customs were being swept away while their economic security was being undermined by the replacement of leases with tenancies at will. Butt's plea to convert tenants into proprietors was widely supported throughout Ireland.[34] This step had long been the goal of the Irish Tenant League, founded in 1850, and was supported by the Irish clergy as well.[35] However, English parliamentarians were by no means convinced.

The idea of property as an absolute right was deeply entrenched in the psyche of the British political elite. Most lawyers saw governmental interference with property rights as permissible only when necessary to provide public services such as securing a right of way for a railroad.[36] Parliament, if anything, was more outspoken in the defense of property rights. Landlords comprised a majority of parliament well into the 1880s. However, representatives of the middle class were equally vocal on the subject. John Bright, for example, thought it "disgusting" that Englishmen could support the demands of the Irish Tenant League.[37] Joseph Hume, otherwise sympathetic to the Irish, saw tenant right as nothing less than communism that "would lead to the robbery of all property."[38]

Given this consensus it was not surprising that parliament offered a solid wall of resistance to measures aimed at redressing agrarian grievances. Down to 1867, for example, all seven bills introduced to compensate tenants for the value of improvements they made were overwhelmingly rejected.

Mill was drawn into this debate as a member of parliament from Westminster, the great citadel of English liberalism. In the two years he served as an M.P., between 1866 and 1868, he took a very active interest in Irish questions. Mill's speeches on the subject were listened to attentively by members of both parties because of his international standing as a philosopher. His debates with Robert Lowe, a particularly articulate spokesman for economic orthodoxy, were one of the political highlights of 1868, the year in which Irish questions dominated the House.[39] Interestingly, Mill was *persona grata* to both radical and more conservative factions within parliament. Each found arguments in his writings that gave support to its point of view. The Irish reformers and their allies had long counted Mill as a member of their camp. Both the *Spectator* and the *Westminster Review* claimed to be advancing Mill's principles in their call for a drastic limitation of the rights of Irish landlords.[40] In 1851, Gavan Duffy, a founder of the Tenant League, had even asked Mill to stand for parliament from an Irish constituency.[41] Conservatives who nevertheless favored gradual progress admired Mill for his balance. They pointed with approval to his defense of property rights and his discussion of the possible adverse effects of democracy upon property, arguments to be found in the *Principles*.

At the height of the 1868 "Irish Session" Mill published his pamphlet *England and Ireland*.[42] Although just forty-four pages it became, in the opinion of R. D. Collison Black, "probably the most influential single contribution to the extended debate on Irish land problems which was carried on in England between 1865 and 1870."[43]

England and Ireland marked another shift, this time a permanent one, in Mill's thought about the Irish land question. In it he finally rejected all halfway measures and advocated decisive state action to transform Ireland into a country of peasant proprietors. The pamphlet progressed directly from the realm of theory to the practical application of that theory, a transition Mill had previously shied away from. There was no evidence of the hesitation and second thoughts that ran through the several editions of the *Principles*. In fact, the *Principles* and the various arguments contained in them were never once alluded to. Mill the pragmatist and Victorian libertarian had finally accepted the compelling logic of Mill the political economist.

Mill's about-face was ultimately the result of a long and tortuous intellectual process, but the immediate catalyst for it was unquestionably the advent of Fenianism and its frightening implications for the future of Anglo-Irish relations. What bothered Mill about the Fenians was the fact that they were not demanding redress of any particular grievances but rather expressing implacable opposition to the very idea of a continued connection with Britain. "What seems to them [the English] the causelessness of the Irish repugnance to our rule," Mill warned, "is the proof that they have almost let pass the last opportunity they are ever likely to have of setting it right. They have allowed what once was indignation against particular wrongs, to harden into a passionate determination to be no longer ruled on any terms by those to whom they ascribe all their evils" (p. 7).

Rebellions of an ideological nature, Mill insisted, are the most difficult to control: "Revolt against practical ill-usage may be quelled by concessions; but wait till all practical grievances have merged in the demand for independence, and there is no knowing that any concession, short of independence, will appease the quarrel" (p. 7). Britain faced such a revolt of nationalism in Ireland, one which Mill lamented might have been prevented if only because it took so long to develop. Despite this pessimistic attitude it is apparent that Mill believed Ireland might still be won over if the British government acted with dispatch to settle once and for all the land question, which still generated the kind of peasant dissatisfaction on which the Fenians prospered.

Mill's treatment of the land question began on a very theoretical plane. His argument was designed to overcome the orthodox opposition to any limitation of property rights by suggesting that the utility of those rights was culture bound. Mill insisted that institutions, to be effective, must suit the character and culture of a people; that it was impractical to transplant the institutions of one country to another. Such a lack of cultural relativism, in his view, lay at the very root of the Irish problem. England was so different in character and history from Ireland yet the British so "conceited" about their institutions that it was almost inevitable they would fail in their attempt to govern Ireland (pp. 8–10).

The most telling example of the evil England had created by importing institutions ill-suited to the character of the people was, of course, the distress caused by the application of the concept of absolute property in land. Absolute property rights were injurious to the general welfare unless they were rooted in the "traditions and oldest recollections of the people; the landed families must be identified with the religion of the country, with its nationality, with its ancient rulers, leaders, defenders, teachers, and other objects of gratitude and veneration, or at least of ungrudging obedience" (p. 11). This was the situation in England but the very opposite of that which prevailed in Ireland.

In Ireland, according to Mill, the tradition of communal ownership was deeply rooted. The feudal idea of all rights coming from the landlord was imposed only after the Conquest and like other importations, most notably Protestantism, it was never recognized by the people and remained associated in their minds with foreign domination. Even so, the institution might have prevailed had the landlord class succeeded in legitimizing the change. Instead, the landlords became a "mere burthen" on the land. "The whole rental of the country was wasted in maintaining, often in reckless extravagance, people who were not nearly as useful to the hive as the drones are, and were entitled to less respect" (pp. 12–13). The management of the land thus continued to be an odious oppression, the repercussions of which were particularly injurious to Ireland, the most agricultural of all European countries with the exception of Russia.

Mill proceeded to contrast English landlords with their Irish counterparts. He asserted that English landlords for the most part managed their estates in a commercial spirit, giving tenants an incentive to make the land more productive. But in Ireland improving tenants were likely to be expelled or have their rents increased; they were given no interest in improving the land, only in running it down in order to extract what profit they could in the short run. "An average Irish landlord," Mill wrote, did "not even put up the fences and farm-buildings" which in England it was the landlord's responsibility to provide. If a tenant erected buildings, fences or drainage ditches that were better than ordinary, there was nothing to prevent the landlord from seizing the result; and "so many landlords even of high rank are not ashamed to do this, that it is evident their compeers do not think it at all disgraceful" (pp. 17–18).

The same law in both countries thus encouraged radically different social and economic conditions. In Britain it functioned to uphold a reasonable and efficient system of agriculture. In Ireland it supported a system of wholesale robbery. It was no wonder that the Irish cotter refused to give his allegiance to a system of laws that only enshrined his oppression.

The solution Mill proposed to this inequity was to give the Irish peasant possession of the land subject to a fixed rent. A government commission would decide what constituted reasonable rent in every circumstance. Mill stressed the importance of making the rent fair: inflated rents would stifle initiative and productivity whereas low rents would encourage the tenant to sublease and live as a "parasite." In order to accelerate the transition to peasant proprietorship Mill also proposed that landlords be given the option of completely severing their connection with Irish land by accepting compensation for the value of their estates (pp. 36–37).

Mill saw the alternatives to such reform as truly frightening. Continuing dissatisfaction in Ireland, he argued, would lead to renewed rebellion supported by volunteers from the Continent and from America (where numerous Irish had settled and prospered). The draconic measures required to suppress such risings and maintain imperial authority would never receive the support of the mass of the English people and were certain to embroil England in conflicts with foreign countries, most notably the United States, which would not tolerate the creation of a Poland across the Irish Sea. England would be compelled to grant independence to Ireland.

Independence, Mill averred, would not put an end to Anglo-Irish problems but might actually make them worse. It would leave a hostile Ireland ready to join any coalition against England in order to settle old scores. Mill wisely foresaw that independence also raised the prospect of civil war between Protestant and Catholic Irish and between Ulster and the rest of Ireland. He predicted that the inevitable sympathy of the English people for the Protestants would draw the government into the conflict which, regardless of the outcome, would further poison relations between the two peoples.

The insuperable problems associated with either repression or independence suggested to Mill that continuing the federation of Ireland to England was the only workable constitutional arrangement. This, of course, was predicated upon Irish reconciliation to the Union. Mill thus made clever use of the carrot and stick to mobilize support for land reform. He attempted to demonstrate the unreasonableness of applying the English law of property to Ireland, and for those who might not be swayed by these philosophical and moral arguments he raised the practical problem of coping with the political consequences of inaction.

The impact of *England and Ireland* was profound. The pamphlet dominated the parliamentary debate on the land question. Its arguments probably convinced a number of M.P.'s of the necessity of supporting reform. It may even have been ultimately responsible for Gladstone's Land Reform Acts of 1870. This milestone legislation, together with the Land Act of 1880, secured temporary tranquility for Ireland. But as Mill's critics predicted, land reform did so at a certain cost to agricultural efficiency. Ireland became a country of small farms and Irish agriculture to this day remains among the least productive in Europe. In fairness to Mill it should be pointed out that no course of action other than the encouragement of peasant proprietorship would have been economically or politically feasible. Moreover, the political promise held out by the Reform Acts was almost realized. Land reform helped to create a level of prosperity never before seen in Ireland and went some distance toward reconciling most Irishmen to some kind of continuing association with England.

The tragedy is that land reform, like every other Irish reform, was too late in coming. Mill himself had feared that this might prove to be the case. If land reform had been introduced in the 1830s or 1840s and the Irish peasants transformed into peasant proprietors, a major grievance would have been redressed. Agrarian outrages and the entire movement for repeal of the Act of Union would have lost their impetus and the Irish people would probably have become reconciled to England. No doubt, much of the suffering caused by the great potato famine could have been averted if reform had been enacted in time. The revolution of 1848 would have been still-born as would the Fenian uprising two decades later. However, land reform was enacted not in 1840 but in 1870 and 1880, and like Catholic Emancipation before it, it was not perceived by the Irish people as a conciliatory gesture but rather as a concession extracted by blood. It was also like Catholic Emancipation in that its effects were in some ways ambiguous. By 1870 the greater efficiency of British agriculture threatened the economic viability of Irish estates and the profits of Irish landowners were declining precipitously. The Land Reform Act enabled these proprietors to leave Ireland at a particularly auspicious time. It also guaranteed that their land would be sold at a price above what it would have fetched on the open market. Accordingly, the act hardly impressed the Irish people with Britain's concern for their well-being.

NOTES

1. These opposing conceptions of Irish agricultural development are treated extensively in R. D. Collison Black, *Economic Thought and the Irish Question, 1817–1870* (Cambridge, 1960). This is by far the most useful book on the relationship between the development of economic thought and the promulgation of policy. Collison Black sees opposition to land reform as arising almost entirely from the tenacity with which Victorians held to their belief in the absolute right to property. This author is impressed by the extent to which such defenses of property rights were often rationalizations for underlying prejudices about the Irish and Ireland. For the development of this argument see Richard Ned Lebow, "British Images of Poverty in Pre-Famine Ireland," in Daniel J. Casey and Robert E. Rhodes, eds., *Views of the Irish Peasantry, 1800–1916* (Hamden, 1977), pp. 57–85; and Lebow, *White Britain and Black Ireland: The Influence of Stereotypes on Colonial Policy* (Philadelphia, 1976).

2. David Ricardo, *Works and Correspondence,* ed. P. Sraffa with M. H. Dobb (10 vols., Cambridge, 1951–55), in particular, *Principles of Political Economy and Taxation,* Chapter 2. Nassau W. Senior, *Two Lectures on Population* (London, 1829); *A Letter to Lord Howick, on a Legal Provision for the Irish Poor*

(2nd ed., London, 1831); *Remarks on Emigration, with the Draft of a Bill* (London, 1831); "An Outline of the Science of Political Economy," in *Encyclopedia Metropolitana* (London, 1836); *Journals, Conversations and Essays Relating to Ireland* (2 vols., London, 1868). Lowe's opinions were expressed in parliamentary debate: see note 39.

3. See, for example, the works of R. Torrens, the most indefatigable publicist for this point of view. Representative selections include *The Colonisation of South Australia* (London, 1835); *Plan of an Association in Aid of the Irish Poor Law* (London, 1838); and *Systematic Colonisation: Ireland Saved, without Cost to the Imperial Treasury* (2nd ed., London, 1849). According to K. H. Connell, *The Population of Ireland, 1780–1845* (Oxford, 1950), there is very little evidence of the consolidation of estates between the end of the Napoleonic Wars and the onset of the famine. One important reason for this was resistance, often violent, put up by Irish tenants to clearances.

4. One of the earliest advocates of fixity of tenure, i.e., a system of *de facto* peasant proprietorship, as a means of coping with the social and economic problems of the Irish countryside was W. Conner. See especially his early writings: *The Speech of William Conner, Esq., against Rack-rents, etc.* (Dublin, 1832); *The True Political Economy of Ireland; or, Rack-rent the One Great Cause of all her Evils, with Its Remedy* (Dublin, 1835); *The Axe Laid to the Root of Irish Oppression; and a Sure and Speedy Remedy for The Evils of Ireland* (Dublin, 1840). An account of Conner's ideas is provided by G. O'Brien, "William Conner," *Studies,* XII (June 1923), pp. 279–89. From 1835 on, the major parliamentary supporter for tenant compensation for improvements was William Sharman Crawford, member from Dundalk and later from Rochdale. Crawford introduced bills in 1835–36, 1843 and 1845 to give evicted tenants compensation for any improvements they had made. In 1846 and 1848 he introduced bills to extend tenant rights throughout Ireland. See his *Defence of the Small Farmers of Ireland,* which originally appeared as a series of ten letters published in the *Northern Whig* (Belfast) between September 10 and October 1, 1839, and was reprinted as a pamphlet the same year in Belfast.

5. 1845 (605), XIX, 1: *Report from Her Majesty's Commissioners of Inquiry into the State of the Law and Practice with Respect to the Occupation of Land in Ireland.* 1845 (606), XIX, 57; (616), XXI, 1; (657), XXI, 1: *Evidence Taken Before Her Majesty's Commissioners of Inquiry into the State of the Law and Practice with Respect to the Occupation of Land in Ireland.*

1845 (672), XXII, 1: (673), XXII, 225: *Appendix and Index to Above Inquiry.*

6. See J. E. Pomfret, *The Struggle for the Land in Ireland* (Princeton, 1930) and Michael Davitt, *The Fall of Feudalism in Ireland* (London, 1904), the latter being a more passionate account by an Irish activist.

7. Crawford's pamphlet has already been cited. Scrope's writings on this subject are extensive. See, for example, *Common Cause of Landlord, Tenant and Labourer* (London, 1833); *How is Ireland to be Governed?* (London, 1846); *Extracts of Evidence . . . on the Subject of Waste Lands Reclamation* (London, 1847); *Letters to Lord John Russell, M.P., etc., on the Further Measures Required for the Social Amelioration of Ireland* (London, 1847). Duffy, the organizer of the Irish Tenant League, spoke out in Parliament. For Butt, see his *Land Tenure in Ireland; A Plea for the Celtic Race* (Dublin, 1866); *Fixity of Tenure; Heads of a Suggested Legislative Enactment; with an Introduction and Notes* (Dublin, 1866); *The Irish People and the Irish Land: A Letter to Lord Lifford* (Dublin, 1867).

8. Friedrich von Raumer, *England in 1835,* trans. H. E. Lloyd (3 vols., London, 1836); Gustave de Beaumont, *Ireland Social, Political and Religious,* ed. W. Cooke Taylor (London, 1839).

9. John Stuart Mill to Gustave D'Eichtal, March 11 and May 15, 1829, in *The Earlier Letters of John Stuart Mill, 1812–1848,* ed. Francis E. Mineka (2 vols., Toronto, 1963), nos. 24 and 26.

10. *Ibid.,* John Stuart Mill to Gustave D'Eichtal, October 8, 1829, no. 27; to Alexis de Tocqueville, January 7, 1837, no. 185.

11. John Stuart Mill, *Principles of Political Economy, with Some of their Applications to Social Philosophy* (1st ed., London, 1848). The variorum edition appears in *Collected Works of John Stuart Mill* (Toronto, 1963–), vols. II and III. This is the edition cited throughout.

12. *Principles,* II, p. 230.

13. *Ibid.,* II, pp. 224–26, 228–29.

14. *Ibid.,* II, p. 231.

15. Arthur Young, *A Tour in Ireland: With General Observations on the Present State of that Kingdom, 1776–1779* (Dublin, 1780).

16. See notes 40 and 41.

17. For a detailed analysis of the differences in Mill's views on the land question in successive editions, see E. D. Steele, "J. S. Mill and the Irish Question: The Principles of Political Econ-

omy, 1848–1865," *Historical Journal,* XIII (1970), pp. 216–36. Steele's *Irish Land and British Politics: Tenant-Right and Nationality, 1865–1870* (Cambridge, 1974) is also a very useful book on the background to the Land Act of 1870. See especially Chapter 2.

18. *Principles,* II, pp. 225–28.

19. *Ibid.,* pp. 22–33.

20. *Ibid.*

21. W. T. Thornton, *Over-population, and Its Remedy* (London, 1846) and *A Plea for Peasant Proprietors, with the Outlines of a Plan for Their Establishment in Ireland* (London, 1848). Mill frequently refers to Thornton in both his *Morning Chronicle* articles and *England and Ireland.*

22. See Michael St. John Packe, *The Life of John Stuart Mill* (New York, 1954), p. 296, which states that Mill had the privilege to contribute leaders to the *Morning Chronicle* during the duration of the famine. He stopped in January 1847, when he felt that the staff of the newspaper had sufficiently mastered the theme to continue without his assistance. Mill acknowledged that his main interest in writing these articles was to encourage the government to reclaim Irish wastelands and parcel them out in small properties among the peasantry. John Stuart Mill to Alexander Bain, December 28, 1846, and to Henry S. Chapman, March 9, 1847, *The Earlier Letters of John Stuart Mill,* nos. 494 and 499.

23. *Principles,* II, pp. 225–28.

24. Nassau Senior, "Relief of Irish Distress in 1847 and 1848," *Edinburgh Review,* LXXXIX (1849), reprinted in *Journals, Conversations and Essays Relating to Ireland,* I, p. 257.

25. See Collison Black, *Economic Thought and the Irish Question,* Chapters 6 and 7. A wastelands bill was brought in by Lord John Russell in 1847 but met with strong opposition in Commons. In response, the government reduced the sum it proposed to appropriate from £1 million to £500,000 and then dropped the scheme altogether.

26. *Ibid.,* p. 180ff.

27. Quoted in J. C. Beckett, *The Making of Modern Ireland, 1603–1923* (New York, 1966), p. 353.

28. Parliament rejected all Irish reform measures with respect to land, even those bills designed to reduce Irish pressures by making the most meager concessions. See Steele, *Irish Land and British Politics,* Chapter 2.

29. *Principles,* 5th ed. (1862), Chapters 9 and 10.

30. *Ibid.,* p. 184.

31. See J. O'Leary, *Recollections of Fenians and Fenianism*

(2 vols., London, 1896) and J. Devoy, *Recollections of an Irish Rebel* (London, 1929) for source material on the Fenians. See also the discussion in Beckett, *The Making of Modern Ireland,* pp. 358–62.

32. Beckett, p. 362.

33. See footnote 7 for a list of Butt's publications.

34. See the discussion in Collison Black, *Economic Thought and the Irish Question,* pp. 52–53, citing the position and influence of the *Freeman's Journal* on the question of fixity of tenure.

35. The clergy had long been associated with advancing tenant rights and one of the principal figures in the Irish Tenant League was Richard O'Brien, the Catholic Dean of Limerick. Even the more conservative bishops, most notably David Moriarty, Bishop of Kerry, supported the demands for compensation and fixity of tenure. See Collison Black, p. 53, citing a letter from Moriarty to Butt.

36. See Steele's discussion of this problem, in *Irish Land and British Politics,* pp. 36–37.

37. John Bright to Richard Cobden, October 12, 1850. Bright Papers (43383), cited in Steele, *ibid.,* p. 36.

38. *Hansard's Parliamentary Debates* (3rd series, London, 1831–50), CXIX, col. 346, February 10, 1842.

39. *Ibid.,* CXC; this volume contains the Irish debate.

40. *Spectator* article cited in Steele, *Irish Land and British Politics,* p. 53; "Tenant-Right in Ireland," *Westminster Review,* July 1868.

41. See Packe, *Life of John Stuart Mill*, pp. 325–26.

42. It was issued in London by Longmans, Green, Reader and Dyer.

43. Collison Black, *Economic Thought and the Irish Question,* p. 53.

EDITORIALS
from the
MORNING
CHRONICLE

John Stuart Mill

[The following are selections from Mill's unsigned editorials (leaders) in the *Morning Chronicle* of London. For the attribution of these articles to Mill, see especially Ney MacMinn, J. R. Hainds, and James McNab McCrimmon, eds., *Bibliography of the Published Writings of John Stuart Mill* (Evanston, Ill., 1945), pp. 60-61, 64. Also see, for example, Michael St. John Packe, *The Life of John Stuart Mill* (New York, 1954), p. 296; Eugene August, *John Stuart Mill: A Mind at Large* (New York, 1975), p. 108; and the essay in this volume by Richard Ned Lebow, p. 8. The initialed footnotes to the following pages are by Dr. Lebow.]

SATURDAY, OCTOBER 10, 1846

THE GRAND economical evil of Ireland is the cottier-tenant system. We were on the point of calling it the grand moral evil also. Neither the economical nor the moral evils admit of any considerable alleviation while that baneful system continues.

This truth is the foundation of the philosophy of Irish wretchedness and Irish improvement. It is the one thing to be known, remembered, and perpetually thought of by all who concern themselves about that country. It is the conclusion which almost every one who sincerely and seriously applies his mind to the matter ends by aiming at. There is hardly any road whereby a conscientious thinker can approach the subject of Irish distress which does not lead directly to it.

But it is not always clearly seen in what the radical mischief of this tenure, as it exists in Ireland, consists. It is often confounded with the evil of small holdings. Holdings certainly may, under any system, be too small. But there may be small holdings without a cottier system; and there may be a cottier system without small holdings.

A cottier system may be defined, that in which the produce of the land is divided between two sharers—a landlord on one side, and labourers on the other; the competition of the labourers being the regulating principle of the division. To see this system in the fulness of its pernicious fruits, two other circumstances must be supposed, both of which pre-eminently exist in Ireland:—a country over-peopled, at least in proportion to the efficiency of its industry, and no considerable outlet for labour, otherwise than in agriculture.

In all countries in which the labouring population have no property, their condition depends upon the intensity of the competition for employment. In England, and most civilized countries, the pressure of this competition is upon capital; in Ireland, under the cottier system, it is upon land. In England, over population produces its effect by lowering wages; in Ireland, by raising rent.

Now, there is a truth so universally borne out by experience as almost to partake of the character of a law of nature; and it is this. Whenever a population, excessive in proportion to the productive power of its industry, depends for subsistence wholly upon the occupancy of land, their competition drives them to offer for the land a rent merely nominal, a rent greater than the utmost which, even on the most favourable supposition, they can possibly pay. A farmer who has capital, who brings something to the farm, and risks something upon it, will not bind himself to a higher rent than he thinks he can pay without, at all events, encroaching on his capital. A labourer who bids for land, not for the sake of profit, but for subsistence, and with whom not to have land is to be without the means of living, will offer anything rather than be outbid by his neighbour. In such a case, if there is any limit to the nominal amount of rent, it is to be found, not in the calculations of the tenant, but in the moderation of the landlord, his justice, humanity, or enlightened perception of self-interest.

This is well understood in the East. In India, as in Ireland, there is a superabundant population depending wholly on land. In India, as in Ireland, the people will promise to pay anything for the land rather than not obtain it. The owner of the land therefore, who in India is generally the Government, has long since discovered that it will not do to leave the matter to competition; that itself, as landlord, must not ask the tenant what he *will* pay, but must determine for him what he *can* pay, and resolutely abstain from asking more; that if it has inadvertently asked too much, it must not hold the tenant to his contract, but at once cancel it, and grant another; that this is its interest, even in the narrowest and most selfish acceptation; that in the long run (and not a very long run either) it gets more rent by this mode of proceeding than by any other. Not the English

Government in India only, but all tolerably-administered Native governments, have been taught this wisdom by experience.

The Irish landlords have not generally had this wisdom. Improvident and reckless themselves, needy and indebted, and therefore, by a sort of necessity, rapacious, they have never known how to part with even the shadow of a present gain for the sake of a more certain gain in the future. Many of them, too, preferred increase of power even to increase of income; and were not unwilling that their tenant should enter into engagements which they knew he could not fulfill. They therefore permitted and encouraged rent to grow up, under the impulse of competition, to the point of impossibility. They were thus enabled in all seasons, good or bad, to take everything which the tenant had, except a bare subsistence—and what those words mean in Ireland, we know; and as even then there was always a balance due, the tenant being in the landlord's debt was in the landlord's power, and could at all times, as far as law was concerned, be ejected at pleasure. The various Parliamentary inquiries into the state of Ireland have elicited the fact that tenants have not only covenanted to pay, but actually paid to the landlord more than the whole produce of the land they rented. Their earnings by English harvest work went chiefly to the landlord; and in the small portion of Ireland in which the peasants follow a double trade as agriculturists and weavers, they have been known to pay to the landlord part of their earnings as weavers, in addition to the whole produce of their plot of land;—so intense was the association in their minds between being without land and destitution, so uncontrollable the wish to retain at all costs a hold on some corner of earth, upon which, if other resources failed, they could fall back, and claim that ration of potatoes which any landlord must leave them, since, to pay any rent at all, it is necessary that the tenant should be alive.

We believe that the evil of nominal rents is now generally felt among the Irish landlords themselves, and that those who do not let their lands by competition, or at rack rents, are a constantly increasing proportion. But so long as anything in rent is arbitrary, under a cottier system, the tenant is never secure against the caprice or the necessities of his landlord. The curse of this system is, that it destroys, more utterly than any other system of nominally free labour, all motive either to industry or to prudence. To what end should the tenant, who is hopelessly in arrear to his landlord, exert himself to raise a larger produce? There would only be the more for the landlord to take from him; and one case in ten of its being actually taken is more than enough, since it is well known how small a doubt in a person's mind of his being suffered to enjoy what he earns suffices, when conspiring with the natural indolence of man, to prevent him from earning it. Of what consequence to him is it whether he has only two children or ten? The ten are sure of having their meal of potatoes while there are any on the farm, and if there were but two they would have no more. A people have been for half a thousand years under such a *régime* as this, and men wonder at them for their indolence, and their want of enterprise, and their improvident marriages. They must be something more than human if they were not, in these particulars, all that they are charged with being. But to tell us in all gravity, that because they are all this, therefore they are so by nature and because of a difference of race, is a thing which might rouse the indignation even of persons not very quickly moved to such a sentiment, if that were a proper object of indignation which is perhaps only an aberration of the intellect.

A cottier-tenant system is essentially an anarchical system. Habitual disaffection to the law is almost inherent in it. The Russian people are not more completely separated into serfs and the masters of serfs, than the Irish people into the cultivators and the owners of land—

two classes standing out with interest distinctly and absolutely contrary, and in a position which to the minds of the more numerous class *cannot* seem to be other than that of robbers and the robbed. The Many occupy and till the land, and a few, because they have the power, take from them the greater part of the produce. In England the labourer comes into direct collision of interest only with the farmer, and *he* gives something for what he receives—he gives his capital: even the landlord in England gives for the rent some equivalent to the farmer—he gives the land, enriched by former expenditure of capital—the landlord's own, or that of previous farmers. But what does the Irish landlord give? There are many exceptions, we know, as there are many and honourable exceptions to every thing which has ever been said truly to the discredit of the class. But as a general fact, the Irish landlord gives no equivalent for his rent; he takes and appropriates it, not because he has done anything for the land, but his ancestor seized it, or had it given to him by somebody who did. The right of the Irish landlord to his rent is only that of prescription; a valid title, but one which it is extremely difficult to commend to those who do not profit by it. That a tenantry like the Irish should connect any sacredness with the rights of landlords is simply an impossibility; and it is only the engrossing nature, for centuries past, of the quarrels about religion which has postponed the breaking out of the permanent and irreconcileable quarrel which such a people must always have with the right to land.

The quarrel, however, has been always going on, and has long been a principal feature in the state of Ireland; but there has hitherto been a limit to the demands of the weaker side. They have not said that they would have the land itself, but they have said that they would and should have leave to grow potatoes on it; and they have made their words good by assassinating those who turned them out, or those who accepted after them the place from which they were turned. Such is the cottier system. Idle-

ness and indigence are its elder children; Rockism* its
younger. There is another and a younger, still unborn,
and that other is, Confiscation.

TUESDAY, OCTOBER 13, 1846

AS NO IMPROVEMENT in Ireland, worthy of the name, is
compatible with the cottier system—as all schemes of
Irish regeneration, which are not the merest mockery of
Irish evils, must propose some means of superseding and
extirpating that form of tenancy—so neither have we
been without suggestions, more or less systematic and
matured, which have had this extirpation for their direct
object. Two of these have excited much attention, and
may be said to have deserved it, since, whatever other
objections they are liable to, they would be, or might be,
efficacious for their particular design. One of them has
been more particularly an English scheme, the other an
Irish. The one proposes to alter the agricultural economy
of Ireland by means of the introduction of English capital; the other by establishing what has been called fixity
of tenure. To begin with the first.

The cottier system, say some, has its origin in want of
capital. The labourer must work out his subsistence for
himself from the land, because there is no farmer with
capital to pay him wages. For the same reason the land
goes unimproved, the culture is slovenly, and the tools
are of the rudest description. Ireland has no capital; and
the disturbed state of Ireland prevents English capital
from flowing in. England has superfluous wealth, which
pours itself forth to every other part of the known and
habitable earth. Ireland alone receives no share of this
abounding overflow. Make Ireland tranquil, make life

*Rockism was one of the early names for what later became known
as Ribbonism—combinations among the peasantry to deter landlords
from such practices as rack renting and clearances. —R.N.L.

and property secure, and the spirit of enterprise, for which the world is not sufficiently wide, will no longer avoid one-third part, and that third the most fertile part, of the United Kingdom. But with capital comes employment for labour; with English farming, the social system of the English rural districts would come in; the cottier system would give way before another more enlightened, and more conducive to the interests of all; and in time Ireland, like prosperous England, would have her landlords, her farmers, and her labourers maintained by wages, instead of having only landlords, and labourers maintaining themselves by potato cultivation on little plots of earth.

There is nothing palpably absurd or impossible in this train of supposed consequences, and this plan was for many years the favourite dream of amateur English philanthropists who interested themselves for Ireland. It had the happy recommendation of holding up England and things English as the standard of excellence for all the world. In institutions and social arrangements comparatively little had then occurred to disturb on this point our habitual national self-complacency. The "English cottager" was in those days looked upon as that type of rustic felicity which he is even now held to be by those lady-travellers, and gentlemen-travellers also, who favour the world with printed narratives of their first continental tour. At that time there were not many people to whom the reflection occurred, that a population might be fed on wages and still be wretchedly ill off; nor was it doubted but that the self-indulgent, *sans-souci* Irish potato-digger would rush eagerly to change places with the anxious, care-worn, and not much better fed Dorsetshire labourer, the very instant that the blessed opportunity was afforded to him. Time and better knowledge have considerably modified the general opinion of England on this among many points.

But there is another reason which has contributed still more to bring into discredit the theory which looked for

the cure of Irish economical evils from what was called
the improvement of Irish agriculture. Improvement in
the English sense, improvement by the more powerful
instruments and processes of capitalist-farmers, though
it raises a far greater net produce than the Irish system,
yet from its very nature employs fewer hands. For a
time, therefore, its sole tendency is to aggravate the evil
which it is expected to cure. Its ultimate effects need not
here be entered upon. We may grant that its increased
efficiency and economy, the far greater ratio which its
produce bears to the smaller quantity of labour em-
ployed, the large profits it yields, and the means and
motives which it consequently holds out to accumula-
tion, may in time enable the country to raise a larger
gross produce, and to maintain, therefore, a larger population than could ever exist on the system of small holdings and peasant-farmers. This is one of the long dis-
puted questions which political economists and practical
agriculturists have not yet settled among themselves.
Their opinions on the subject diverge, widely and with
bigotry. But about the immediate effects there is not and
cannot be any difference. The introduction of English
farming is another word for the clearing system. It must
begin by ejecting the peasantry of a tract of country from
the land they occupy, and handing it over *en bloc* to a
capitalist-farmer. The number of those whom he would
require to retain as labourers would be far short of the
number he displaced. What becomes of the remainder?
The increased net produce of the land, when "improved,"
may create a demand for more labour; but what is to be
done in the meantime? And when the demand came, it
would be in great part for manufacturing, not agricultural labour, to supply, not the necessities, but the com-
forts and luxuries of the affluent farmers. But Ireland
has little besides agricultural labour, and the displaced
cottiers are capable of no other. Compared with what we
should then see, all we have yet seen of the clearing
system and its horrors is a bagatelle. No one has seen

the systematic unpeopling of estates on the scale necessary for introducing a system of farming by hired labour.
What we have seen, and on a small number of estates
only, has been intended not to abolish cottier tenancies,
but merely to correct in some degree that extreme subdivision under which, after feeding the cottier and his
family, there was hardly anything remaining for rent.

We shall here state at once our opinion, in plain terms,
respecting this clearing system, by which a population,
which has for generations lived and multiplied on the
land, is, on the plea of legal rights, suddenly turned adrift
without a provision, to find a living—where there is no
living to be found. It is a thing which no pretence of private right or public utility ought to induce society to tolerate for a moment. No legitimate construction of any
right of ownership in land, which it is for the interest of
society to permit, will warrant it. We hold at the same
time, that to prevent the growth of a redundant population on an estate is not only not blameable, but is one of
the chief duties of a landowner having the power over his
tenants which the Irish system gives. As it is his duty, so
it is, on any extended computation, his pecuniary interest. He is to be commended for *preventing* overpopulation,
but to be detested for tolerating first, and then extermi-
nating it. Society may suffer the thing to be done by one
landlord, or by two or three, without interfering otherwise than by a moral stigma; because the sufferers, having a large surface to spread over, may obtain relief by
employment, or charity: and for another reason—there
are many powers useful to society in the main, but susceptible of such perversion as would render them unen-
durable evils. One of these is the free disposal of land by
the landowner. These powers society permits to exist, but
reserves to itself a liberty of interference in extreme
cases. Any extension of the system of clearing such that
the destitution produced would rise to the magnitude of a
social evil, constitutes such an extreme case; and if society failed in the imperative duty of interference, it is a

satisfaction to reflect, lawless and anti-social as the alternative is, that there is a force of resistance in human beings, in the last resort, which does not always suffer the extreme of injustice to be consummated with safety to the perpetrators. "Captain Rock"* and his family have solved the question of Irish clearances. They have made it, and will continue to make it, impracticable to abolish the cottier system by the simple plan of abolishing the lives of the cottiers themselves.

WEDNESDAY, OCTOBER 14, 1846

AT THAT one brief period in its long existence in which the Repeal Association condescended to give to the real evils of Ireland a place, though but a secondary one, in its list of complaints and grievances—at that rare and long-waited-for moment in its history when its discussions and its agitation held out for the first time some promise of being useful, and therefore in the eyes of a certain sort of people some threat of being dangerous, and which Sir ROBERT PEEL accordingly selected for his well-judged attempt to put down the Association by the hands of law, thereby stopping the good, though not the evil, which it had begun to set in motion—the English people, and especially the landed and propertied classes, were startled from their propriety by the new and ominous sound of Fixity of Tenure.

These words express a mode of abolishing cottier tenancy, the reverse, in all respects, of the clearing system; the reverse in practice, and still more decidely contrary in theory. For while the one recognises no rights in anybody connected with the land save him whom the law denominates its owner, and treats those whose hands till it as if they were created for it, and it for the

*The nickname of one of the peasant leaders. See earlier note on Rockism. —R.N.L.

landlord; the other proceeds upon a view of the relative moral rights of these classes—strange, we must allow, and paradoxical to minds bred in the traditions of English social economy. It actually maintains, that when a hundred families and their ancestors for many generations have cultivated certain lands, and received therefrom the smallest share of the produce on which they could live, and one family and its ancestors have during the same period done nothing to the land, except consume in idleness all the rest of what has been produced by the hundred—if things at any time come to such a pass between the hundred families and the one family as that either one or the other must quit, this theory, which calls itself Fixity of Tenure, dares actually assert that it is the one and not the hundred who ought to depart; that let the law say what it will, when we come to the root of the matter, the hundred have the best *claim* to be there *in foro conscientiae*, and on the substantial principles of right and wrong; and that it is the duty of the Legislature to make its laws accord with those supreme principles.

The scheme, in short, is to protect the tenantry against being ever turned out for the mere pecuniary interest of the landlord, and against ever having their rent raised beyond what is paid at present, or what would be fixed by an impartial arbitrator as the present value of the land. The owner is considered entitled to his rent, but to his rent alone; not to any power over the tenant—power extending to taking away his livelihood; and not even to any increase of rent. The present rent would be fixed for ever as a quit-rent. Subject to that fixed annual payment, the property in the land would in truth be transferred to the tenant; the present landlords no longer owning the land itself, but a rent-charge payable from its produce.

The objections to this scheme are so obvious, that justice has never been done, on this side of the Irish Channel, to its merits. It is a real and a thorough remedy. It goes to the very root of Irish evils. In place of the worst economical system that afflicts any country not cursed with actual slavery, it would substitute the very best of which a country like Ireland is susceptible. It would give to Ireland the inestimable blessing of a peasant proprietary. Give them fixity of tenure, and they would thenceforth work and save for themselves alone. Their industry would be their own profit; their idleness would be their own loss. If they multiplied imprudently, it would be at their own expense, no longer at the expense of the landlords. Here is the secret for converting an indolent and reckless into a laborious, provident, and careful people. It is a secret which never fails. All over Europe, the untiring labourer, the peasant whose industry and vigilance never sleep, is he who owns the land he tills. Labours are executed by peasant proprietors such as are seen no where else, as it would be irrational to expect anywhere else. It would never answer to a farmer or a landlord to pay wages to any one for doing what a peasant proprietor will do on his own ground, and call it not labour but pleasure. All over Europe too, wherever the increase of population is slow, not from legal restraints but from individual prudence, as in France, Switzerland, Norway, it is in countries of peasant proprietors.

The mischiefs which are to be set against these advantages are not on the side of the people, but of the landlords. The plan of fixity of tenure would be unjust to them, unless compensation were made to them for the present value of the future increase of rent which they might expect from the ordinary progress of society. The power which they would be deprived of is not a proper subject of compensation. Power in one human being over others must be presumed to exist for other purposes than the pleasure or benefit of the person possessing it, and any complaint of personal injury in being deprived of it should be hooted out of court with ignominy. Still, however, the change would be a violent disturbance of legal rights, amounting almost to a social revolution, though not greater than that which has been effected in Prussia, amidst the applauses of Europe, by the edicts of an absolute Sovereign. To enlightened foreigners, to von RAUMER or GUSTAVE DE BEAUMONT, the thing appears so natural and obvious, that they are hardly able to account for its not having yet been done. But to those who understand the fixed habits of thought, and artificial feelings stronger than nature itself, which must be broken through before an English legislature could sanction so drastic a process; and who appreciate the danger of tampering, in times of political and moral change, with the salutary prepossessions by which property is protected against spoliation; a measure like this must be looked upon as an extreme remedy, justifiable only as remedies even more revolutionary would be justifiable if there existed no other means of overcoming evils like those of Ireland.

Our conviction, however, is, that those evils are not to be remedied by anything less than the creation of a numerous peasant proprietary. Property in the soil has a sort of magic power of engendering industry, perseverance, forethought in an agricultural people. Any other charm for producing those qualities we know not of, and should be thankful to any one who could point one out. All other schemes for the improvement of Ireland are schemes for getting rid of the people. The very best is a gigantic plan of emigration, impracticably costly, yet, if executed, having no guarantee in the altered relations of society that those left behind would not soon be as miserable as ever. No such guarantee is possible but by making an effectual change in the motives of conduct operating upon the people themselves. There is no known means of working that change but by creating peasant proprietors. Happily, however, it is not necessary for the end in view that the whole peasantry should be owners of land. It is enough if there be a large class, objects of emulation to all the rest, and among whom no one who exerts himself need despair of being numbered. The one measure of practicable improvement for Ireland is to form such a class, and the obvious resource for this purpose is the waste lands.

THURSDAY, OCTOBER 15, 1846

Two miles from the little town of Kilcullen, in Kildare, is a tract of excessively green land, dotted over with brilliant white cottages, each with its couple of trim acres of garden, where you see thick potato ridges covered with blossom, great blue plots of comfortable cabbages, and such pleasant plants of the poor man's garden. Two or three years since the land was a marshy common, which had never since the days of the Deluge fed any being bigger than a snipe, and into which the poor people descended, draining and cultivating, and rescuing the marsh from the water, and raising their cabins, and setting up their little enclosures of two or three acres upon the land which they had thus created. There are now two hundred flourishing little homesteads upon this rescued land, and as many families in comfort and plenty. Now, if two or three acres of reclaimed marsh can furnish plentiful subsistence to one family, 600,000 acres would do as much for 200,000 families; that is to say, for one-fourth part of the Irish peasantry, which is as large a proportion as can well be supposed unable to procure a competent livelihood. According to the most recent accounts, there are considerably more than six millions of acres of land lying waste in Ireland, of which about three-fifths are acknowledged to be improvable.

THIS PASSAGE is from the work of Mr. WILLIAM THORNTON, "Over-population and its Remedy;" a book honourably distinguished from most others of recent date, by the union of philanthropic feelings with sound knowledge and good sense. We recommend the whole work, and particularly its opinions and recommendations on Irish affairs, to the consideration of those who have any power over the present critical turning point in the destinies of that ill-treated country.

Mr. FOSTER'S* indolent Celt, then, is not incapable of enterprise and persevering industry, when the object which calls forth those qualities lies in the direction of his previous habits. He is already an improver and reclaimer of waste lands; nay, he is almost alone in that character. Mr. NICHOLLS† states, that most of the recently recovered bog which he saw in his journey through the western counties was reclaimed, not by the landlords, but by small occupiers, who drained and enclosed an acre or two at a time. This they did without even the motive of property; knowing that they could not thereby acquire a title to the land; knowing that the best which they could expect would be to hold the ground rent free, until the landlord's or his agent's sense of justice had exhausted itself with the degree of forbearance shown them. Squatters are, we have reason to think, by no means unfrequent on Irish estates. These people reclaim and cultivate the waste, well knowing that they shall have rent to pay, and that ultimately they shall only be permitted to hold the land which they have rendered productive, on the same footing as other cottiers. But they hope for a few years' respite. They hope to be allowed to make the land worth taking before the landlord steps in and takes it. They hope that he will for a few years connive at their doing his work, at their supporting themselves by the land while they render it capable of afterwards affording rent to him.

The fact, then, being established, that the waste can be reclaimed by the peasantry themselves, even from a less motive than a property in it, and without any assistance

---

*T. C. Foster, the "Commissioner" in Ireland for *The Times,* attributed Irish poverty to defects in the Irish character, especially laziness.—*R.N.L.*

†Sir George Nicholls was appointed the first Commissioner of the Irish Poor Law in 1836 and later published *A History of the Irish Poor-Law* (London, 1856). —*R.N.L.*

from the State, one would think the most obvious idea
which could present itself to any one who wished to use
the waste lands as an instrument for improving the condition of the peasantry, would be to make that which already takes place on a small scale take place on a large,
by giving to the peasantry the inducement of property in
the soil reclaimed by them, and by affording to them,
from the State, such assistance as may be needful, and as
the State is willing to give. The assistance required would
cost less to the State than the most moderate sum ever
voted by Parliament for Irish distress. That the bogs and
mountains of Ireland may sometimes be drained and enclosed without capital, is proved by the fact that the thing
is already done. It often requires nothing but labour—a
commodity of which Irish cottiers have always more than
enough on their hands. It would be necessary to buy up
the rights of those who are now the nominal owners of
these lands; for there can be no more than nominal
ownership of that which has never been used since the
country was inhabited, and cannot be used now unless the
State supplies the means. The value of an Irish bog is only
the value of the right to cut turf on it. Having become the
proprietor of the whole or a sufficient portion of the waste,
the State could divide it into portions of the most conve-
nient size, and grant these in absolute property to such of
the peasantry as could produce the best certificates of
steadiness and industry, or to such as would undertake to
bring their lots into cultivation with the smallest amount
of pecuniary assistance. If it were necessary to advance to
each family a year's food, and a trifle for tools, where
would be the difficulty? The interest of this, laid on in the
form of a perpetual quit-rent, would save the State from
loss, and would be but a small abatement from the value
of the boon; or instead of a perpetual, the State might
receive its compensation in the form of a terminable an-
nuity, so as ultimately to enfranchise the land from all
payment. In cases in which it would be desirable to oper-
ate on a greater scale, by draining at once the whole of a

large tract of country, the State can as easily do this for the peasantry as Lord BESSBOROUGH* can now undertake to do it for the landlords. The work, during its execution, would provide food and employment for the famishing people in the one way as effectually as in the other, and the State could be indemnified by an additional quit-rent, payable from the new peasant proprietors.

By this plan one-fourth or one-third of the Irish peasantry would, in two or three years, be not only in a state of present ease, but under the influence of the strongest attainable motives to industry, prudence, and economy, and with their interests all ranged on the side of tranquillity and the law, because the law would have ceased to be their oppressor, and become their benefactor. Nor would the benefit stop here. The remaining peasantry, and the landlords themselves, would be only a degree less benefitted than the new proprietary. That clearance of estates which is now synonymous with turning out the population to starve, and which, precisely because it *ought* not, *cannot* be effected save on the most inconsiderable scale while things remain as at present, would then accomplish itself spontaneously, and with unmixed benefit, by the mere withdrawing of a large section of the people from the competition for land. The residuary population would not be too numerous to be supported, in comparative comfort, yet leaving a large rent for the landlord; and English capital and English farming might *then* be introduced with advantage to all, because the cottier population would no longer exceed the numbers who could, with benefit to the farmer, be retained on the land as labourers. Then, and then only, would English capital find its way to Ireland, for then, and only then, would its owner have nothing to fear from the "wild justice" of an ejected tenantry. That tenantry would exist no more as tenantry, but they would exist as farm labourers; not such as the

*In July 1846 Lord Bessborough had been appointed Lord Lieutenant of Ireland by the Russell government.

Wiltshire or Dorsetshire labourer, without heart because without hope, with nothing which he can rise to, nothing to reward or encourage exertion and self-denial, but a prize of two sovereigns from an agricultural society, and the poor-house for his sole ultimatum and harbour of refuge. Not such would the Irish peasant be, but cheered and stimulated by the hope which animates the Continental labourer, the hope of being in time numbered, through industry and frugality, among the class of peasant proprietors; a lot sufficiently above his own to be desirable, and not sufficiently so to be unattainable.

WEDNESDAY, OCTOBER 21, 1846

IN ANOTHER COLUMN will be found a letter, signed "N.," called forth by the observations in our paper of the 14th, on fixity of tenure. The writer charges us with recommending, "openly and without disguise, the doctrine of general spoliation," as applied to the landowners of Ireland; with advising "glibly and smoothly, that a general confiscation of the landed property of a whole country shall take place, and that what now belongs to the landlord by a right as good as that by which any man holds the coat that covers his back, shall henceforward be transferred to the tenant."

When at a moment the most critical perhaps in Irish history, either for good or for evil, we endeavoured, so far as in us lay, that the abundance of good and honest feeling which now exists in the English Government and public towards Ireland, might not run to sheer waste for want of thought; when on the first occasion upon which such an exposition had a chance of being listened to, we showed, as others before us had shown without effect, what is really the root of Irish evils, how deep into the structure of Irish society the remedy, if it is to be really a remedy, must penetrate, and yet how easy, simple, and obvious it is, if they on whom it depends would only have the courage to think so; when we commenced this task, which we have not done without full conviction of the truth of the principles we have advanced, and a firm determination to stand by them to the utmost while that conviction remains unshaken, we were fully prepared to expect that for some time our opinions and purpose would not only be perversely misrepresented, but in many cases honestly misunderstood. This is so inevitably the fate of all political ideas beyond the strictest commonplace, as soon as there seems any possibility of their becoming practical, that we should have been disappointed if we had escaped the common lot; since an exemption would have proved to us nothing more flattering than that what we had written, under some hope of being useful, had not had the good fortune to excite any attention.

But although we were prepared for a good deal of misunderstanding, and for a good deal of trouble in setting it right, we did think we had sufficiently guarded against the particular misconception contained in the letter of our correspondent, and which we are still convinced could not have been fallen into by any one who had read our observations with sufficient attention. It is hardly necessary to say to those who have done so, that the plan technically called fixity of tenure is not our plan; we did but pass it in review, as we did other plans, for the purpose of rejecting it. And so little did we deserve our correspondent's animadversions, that after we had pointed out that under certain modifications the scheme would not be a violation of property at all, we rejected it even as so modified, because, though it had not the reality, it would have the appearance of such a violation.

Without, however, occupying the reader any further with what we said formerly, we will say now what we think on the subject. To bind down the landlord in perpetuity to his present rent would be a spoliation of property. It would be a confiscation of his contingent prospects of an increase of income—a contingency which, in any progressive country, and under anything but the most intolerable mismanagement, amounts to a certainty, and which, like any other prospective gain, has its present marketable value. It would mulct him of the difference between the selling price of his land, and the price of a similar income secured on mortgage or in the public funds. Viewed in this light, we disapprove it as decidedly and should oppose it as strenuously as our correspondent, though we certainly did not express ourselves in quite such indignant language, for we confess that, however wrong we think them, we cannot feel any very bitter indignation against those who, where a whole people are the sufferers, propose desperate remedies for desperate diseases.

But we repeat, and we challenge who will to deny it, that the whole injustice of fixity of tenure would be cured by pecuniary compensation, and by a compensation strictly limited to the pecuniary loss. Whatever the estate would lose in saleable value if the rent were converted into a rent-charge, the landlord ought to receive, either from the tenant or from the state, and could not without flagrant injustice be deprived of. Receiving this, he would obtain the full measure of what is thought due to those from whom their land is taken away, often against their strongest protest, for public improvements. That is not accounted plunder, and spoliation, and confiscation. What is not plunder when it affects one person, or ten, or a hundred, is not plunder if applied to five thousand. The number makes no difference in the justice of the case, though it may in the policy, because the magnitude of the transaction brings it into contact with great considerations of public policy, which on the small scale it cannot possibly affect. The general principle is the same in the great case as in the small. The Legislature of the country can deal with the property of the country as expediency requires, making compensation to the owners. This right is recognized by every railroad or canal bill which passes through Parliament. The reform of the social condition of a country is a greater object than any railway bill. If that object could be no other-wise obtained than by treating every landlord in Ireland as railway bills treat all persons through whose property the railway is to be made, we feel assured that our correspondent is not one of those who would be turned back by such an obstacle.

But this measure would be a revolution in itself, and would require for its justification that which justifies a revolution—a state of extreme misgovernment and suffering, otherwise incurable. The first condition is fully realised in Ireland, but the second is not. Milder remedies are possible. This is the point we are labouring to prove, and we call loudly upon our correspondent, and upon those who think with him, to join in our endeavour. For they may be assured, that there is no other mode of permanently averting the extremity which they so justly deprecate. Unless those who have influence in Parliament and in the public can find another remedy, and apply it too, they will not long persuade an uneducated peasantry, who have never yet seen a friend in the law, to respect the proprietary rights which the law gives, when those rights have no sanction in their own feelings; and the choice may soon lie between a real confiscation and a second Cromwellian conquest. The *onus* lies upon every English statesman or publicist, who has an intellect and a conscience, to have an opinion upon what should be given to Ireland *instead of* fixity of tenure; and not only to have án opinion but to express it, and not only to express it but, within his sphere of influence, to act upon it.

In endeavouring to acquit ourselves of our share of this common obligation, we have found it necessary to say that fixity of tenure, though liable as a practical measure to insurmountable objections, has yet one admirable quality, which the greater part of the schemes afloat for Irish improvement have not, and the absence of which makes them so futile and worthless. It gives to the cultivator a permanent interest in the soil. In doing this it combines the greatest economical and the greatest moral good of which Ireland in its present condition is susceptible. And these two things are inseparable; both must be provided for by any plan of improvement deserving the name. Without the moral change, the greatest economical improvement will last no longer than a prodigal's bounty; without the economical change, the moral improvement will not be attained at all. We say therefore, once more, that this feature of the scheme of fixity of tenure must be found in any plan which can be permanently useful to Ireland. The peasantry, or so numerous a class of them as to be an example and a stimulus to the rest, must have somewhere, and under some form, a proprietary interest in the soil. Give them, we say, this proprietary interest in the lands now unoccupied, which, fortunately, are more than sufficient for the purpose, and not only will there be no temptation to encroach on the rights of those who own the cultivated lands, but they will be delivered from an insuperable difficulty and an insupportable burthen, and for the first time will be really masters of the land called theirs. Every class in the country, and almost every individual, would gain, even pecuniarily, by the plan we support. It has no obstacle in men's interests, but only in the timidity and sluggishness of their minds.

The plan, too, has the advantage over fixity of tenure, that while permanent benefit to the Irish people is at the end, the means may be made instrumental to the relief of their immediate necessities. Our correspondent imputes to us very gratuitously a gross absurdity when he says that we "do not explain how, if all the tenants in Ireland were tomorrow to be converted into owners of the patches of ground they occupy, they would be able to raise, by taxation upon themselves, funds to give to themselves wages to save themselves from the famine which at present threatens them." We were not then discussing plans of temporary relief, but of permanent improvement, in which light alone fixity of tenure ever was, or, except by an insane person, ever could be advo-

cated. But the plan we uphold unites both recommenda-
tions. Practised on a sufficient scale, it would at once
expel the acute disease by which Ireland is now afflicted,
and put things in a correct train for permanently cor-
recting her chronic and long-standing malady.

THURSDAY, OCTOBER 22, 1846

THE DUBLIN *Freeman's Journal* of Saturday last, in an
article occasioned by the opinions we have promulgated
respecting the disposal of the waste lands (opinions to
which, as we are pleased, but not surprised, to find, that
influential paper gives its cordial assent), bears the following valuable testimony to the complete practicability
of the reclamation of those lands by peasant labour:—

> A week's ramble through Connemara, or Erris, or
> Kerry, and we presume the same to be true of
> other counties where the waste lands abound, will
> convince the most sceptical that labour can be
> profitably employed in the reclamation even of
> such lands as would not prove remunerative to the
> large capitalist. The Irish peasant's labour was
> hitherto of little value in the market. Labour was
> abundant, employment scarce; and whenever the
> peasant found an opportunity of mingling his la-
> bour with the barren soil, he did so, though with
> no better prospect than that of having the owner
> of the soil come in and possess himself of the per-
> manent fruits of his toil, before he had himself
> reaped even what would pay him a tithe of the
> value of his labour. *We have seen this process re-
> peated many times by the same peasant family.* We
> have seen him reclaim a patch of bog, enjoy it for
> a brief period, and then yield it to a rent-payer;
> *then retire to another patch, to reclaim and yield it
> up in like manner, and so on,* labouring with the
> full conviction that one day or other his lord would

have all the benefit, but ever hoping, even against
experience, that the evil day might be far off. The
peasant family did this because their time was
valueless, and by such a process they were enabled
to make it yield them a sustenance equivalent,
perhaps, to a fifth of its market value. Yet that
fractional payment kept them from begging, and
rendered what would otherwise continue to be barren soil, productive and valuable.

Sic vos non vobis! Are these the purposes for which
landed property is ordained in a country pretending to
civilization? Is it that he who sows may not reap—that
not he who toils, but some other, may receive the benefit? We all know the foundation and justification of the
institution of property to be precisely the reverse. The
moral and social basis of the right of property is the
right of the labourer to the fruits of his labour. All other
proprietary rights exist for the sake of this. The *million-
naire,* who never did a day's work of useful labour with
head or hands, who is society's debtor for everything,
and its creditor for nothing, has his property protected,
not for its own sake, nor for his, but because to meddle
with it would be to violate the right which some ancestor
or predecessor, who *did* work for it, had to transmit it
freely to his descendants, or to persons of his choice. If
all property rests upon no other than this foundation,
landed property does so pre-eminently. Land is not the
produce of labour. No landlord's ancestor made the land.
Why then is land appropriated? We do not mean, why
was it appropriated, for we know that the most usual
ground of possession was force and conquest: but why is
its appropriation rightful? Why is property in land a
recognized necessity of society? On what ground have,
not usurpers and tyrants, but sages and philanthropists,
defended it? On this—that land, although not made by
labour, can only be rendered useful by it, and because
labour will not be applied in the most useful manner by

the exertions of any others than those who have a *permanent interest* in the land.

Land might be held in common, or, what would be less irrational, it might be granted out on yearly leases by the State. It is conceded to individuals in permanent property for one legitimate reason only, because a permanent proprietor has the strongest motive to be an improver. Proprietors exist in order that they may be improvers, not in order that they may profit by improvements made by others. When the proprietors of land, generally speaking, are not improvers, the purposes for which landed property exists are not answered. When, instead of being improvers, they are an obstacle to improvement—when, without any public purpose in view, they keep land waste which others are eager to cultivate, or suffer it to be made valuable by those who have *no* permanent interest in it, in order to seize on the value—we do not say that they are culpable. The law gave them the land, attaching no conditions to the gift, and none but an extraordinary man is a law to himself, according to a higher standard than custom. But we do say that landed property, thus used, exists to frustrate the ends which it is designed to promote. It is instituted that improvement may not be hindered; it exists as the hindrance. It is instituted that what is created by industry may abide with the creators; it exists that what their labour alone has called into being, may be wrung from them.

Seeing what the "indolent Celt" is already found capable of achieving, without the stimulus of property—seeing that the mere prospect of a few years precarious possession has so often induced him, without science, without capital, without aid from the possessors of either, not under the encouragement of law, but in violation of it, with no resource but his own hands, and those of his family, to perform what is regarded as one of the most arduous feats of agricultural improvement, the conversion of peat-bog into arable land; we are justified in believing that if the primeval waste had stood open in the primeval manner to the first occupier, as the prize of him who succeeded in making it valuable, it would long ere this have been covered from one end to the other by a hard-working, frugal, peaceable, and, in all probability, prudent and self-restraining peasant proprietary. Society, which maintains landed property in order that cultivation may thrive, has prevented all this cultivation, by granting to certain persons, over land which they did not use, the power of prohibiting all other persons from using it. What was this done *for?* .What end had society in view in it? What benefit has society reaped from it? What equivalent have its favourites returned to it for the gift? That which was meant as an exclusive right to use the land they have turned into a veto on the use. "Hitherto," in the words of the *Freeman's Journal,* "Irish proprietors almost instinctively looked to the mountains and bogs on their estates as so many grouse-moors and snipe-marshes from which it was their duty to repel the approaches of industry. The Legislature encouraged this sentiment by every possible means, and even seemed to think it a part of its duty to offer every possible obstacle to the introduction of an extended system of improvement."

Let the Legislature, then, repair its error. The rights it has conferred, mischievous and anti-social as they have in fact proved, let it not resume without compensation. Those rights have a market value, and let that value be paid to the last penny. But let it be the present value, not a speculative price, grounded on the improvements which are only to be effected by means of the purchase. The value of the bogs and mountains to their nominal owners is but a trifle. They are entitled to no more; what more the Legislature can spare is required to feed the industrious improvers, while they work for their own future independence, and the State will be amply repaid by a fraction of the value which their labour will bestow on the now worthless land.

WEDNESDAY, DECEMBER 2, 1846

OUR PAPER of Monday contained a set of resolutions by
the guardians of Kilrush Union, in which the Government is urged to devise and carry into effect some plan of
extensive emigration, as a remedy for Irish evils. Kilrush is in the county of Clare, in which one-third of the
adult male population is receiving pauper allowance,
under the name of government employment. No wonder
that the guardians should be anxious to rid themselves
of this terrible incubus, which, if it continues a single
year, bids fair to imbue the whole labouring population
with the feelings of sturdy beggars for the remainder of
the present generation at the least. But it is a wonder
that people should persist for ever in looking five thousand miles off for what they have at their doors. The
Kilrush guardians would not send their sheep or their
oxen across the Atlantic to graze, when there is ample
pasture on the other side of the brook. Why is there a
different rule for human beings? Why so anxious to send
fellow-creatures out of sight, where their success can be
a benefit to nobody but themselves—where no one can be
either taught or inspired by their example? A large body
of the peasantry are to be drafted off and made comfortable, or put in the way of making themselves so, by
giving them land, we suppose, and tools to cultivate it. Is
there any peculiar propriety in selecting the Antipodes
as the scene of this very simple work of justice and be-
neficence? Is the light that is to be kindled one that
should be hid under a bushel? Ought it not rather to be
made to shine before men?

We are as favourable as any one to measures for facilitating emigration. We think that all persons who desire
to remove to the colonies should have every kind of information given them for their guidance, and every
needless difficulty removed from their path. We would
have the system of landed property and the distribution

of population in the colonies so regulated as to afford the greatest possible field of employment for emigrant labour. We would give every facility to the formation of a colonial fund for importing labour from the mother country; and we would even advance for the purpose, from the national treasury, any sum which the colonies desired, and could be expected to repay. We would do everything in aid and support of *voluntary* emigration: but that which is now urged upon the Government is compulsory—for what compulsion is stronger than that in which the alternative is starvation? If nature and necessity created the alternative we should have nothing to say. Nature has hard laws. If there was actually no room for these people in their own country; if at home they must either starve or be supported by alms, under the frivolous pretence of work; if Canada or Australia was the nearest place where it was possible for them to earn a sufficient subsistence by their own labour on land of their own, we should despise the sentimentality which would bid them remain, and be paupers and beggars at home, instead of freemen, citizens, and independent landed proprietors abroad. But they may be all this at home much better than in Australia or Canada—less expensively to the State, and more suitably and advantageously to themselves. We have said it already, and we repeat it—the Celtic Irish are not the best material to colonize with. The English and Scotch are the proper stuff for the pioneers of the wilderness. The life of a backwoodsman does *not* require the social qualities which constitute the superiority of the Irish; it *does* require the individual hardihood, resource, and self-reliance which are precisely what the Irish have not. The first requisite of a backwoodsman is to be able to stand alone, in all senses, physical, intellectual, and moral. He must propose for himself, contrive for himself, execute for himself. He must never need a leader, nor desire a follower. He must be able to turn his hand to everything, and adapt himself summarily to all novelties of situation and circumstance. The Irishman is the opposite of all this. Sympathy and fellowship are indispensable to him. Instead of insisting, John-Bull-like, upon owing everything to himself, the demand of his nature is to be led and governed. He prefers to have some one to lean upon. He has energy and self-will in abundance, because he has strong desires, but it must be in the line of his previous habits and inclinations. He will never emerge from old habits by his own innate force; but he may be guided and persuaded out of them, as many a priest and many a landlord know; for nature and circumstances have so formed the Irish character, that while Irish landlords collectively have been among the worst in Europe, many individual Irish landlords have succeeded in doing with and for their peasantry such things as no English landlord ever did or could do. Such a people are only fit for an old country, and an old country is alone fit for them. Not to add that it is a questionable thing to take a people whom five centuries of misrule have made lawless and disorderly, and plant them down where there cannot possibly be any law or order to restrain them. Even in the United States the Irish are the most riotous and unmanageable part of the population. An Irish peasantry have already graduated but too well in Lynch law.

The fittest place for the Irish peasant is Ireland. It is there that the greatest number of improving influences can be concentrated upon him. Landed property *there* would precisely supply what is wanting to the formation of his character. What is good for him is that all the influences of civilization should be preserved and increased, but that he himself should be gently lifted up and placed *within* the pale, instead of being left outside of it. The possession of property would do this. It would make him an orderly citizen. It would make him a supporter of the law, instead of a rebel against all law but that of his confederacy. It would make him industrious and active, self-helping and self-relying, like his Celtic brother of France. And it would (if anything would) make him, like the same Celtic kinsman, frugal, self-restraining, and provident, both in other things, and in the main article of all, population. These are the natural effects of property, especially landed property, on those who have it, and on those also, almost in an equal degree, who hope to obtain it by exertion and frugality. On our plan every peasant would be either in the one case or in the other. We cannot make them all proprietors; perhaps we would not if we could. But all might have the hope, and, if they chose, the power, of one day becoming so. To remove the surplus labourers is well, but it is well also to do something permanently useful to those who cannot be removed. Their wages, it may be said, would rise. Perhaps they would: undoubtedly so, if the opportunity were taken to get rid of cottier tenure. But very little will have been done for them if they merely look upon these higher wages as convertable into potatoes for a larger number of mouths. The desideratum is, that along with higher wages they should have placed before them an object highly desirable to them, and attainable by saving from their wages. The possession of land would be that object. Of what use is it to create landed properties in New Zealand for Irish peasants, if Ireland is to be given up to cottiers, or even to labourers for hire? Is it so noble a thing, is it an exploit worthy of statesmen and philanthropists, to nurse and cocker up the Irish peasantry with the elevated and enviable condition of Dorsetshire labourers? And this glorious result is the favourite utopianism, the extreme and impracticable ultimatum, of all plans but those which provide a superior class of peasantry, maintained by land and not by wages, in Ireland itself. There is a rather numerous class of regenerators of Ireland who certainly are no visionaries. The ideal of social perfection to which they aspire for her is not pitched high.

We have said nothing on this occasion of the expense of the emigration plan, because enough has been said of

it before, and because the thing really speaks for itself.
We formerly estimated the cost of transporting the
people to Canada, and settling them there, at ten times
the expense of locating them on the waste lands. Others
have since estimated it at thirty times. We know not,
nor is it material, which guess is nearest the truth.
Neither have we spoken of the benefit of employing our
own labour in the improvement of our own country, instead of the improvement of countries which will not
always be ours. These considerations are too obvious to
be missed, and too important to be undervalued. But let
the plan once come to maturity; let its promoters commit
themselves to figures and details, and they will present
us with something either on a scale of palpable insuffi-
ciency (however useful in a distant future), or bearing on
the face of it so lavish a waste of public resources,
squandered irrecoverably (for settlers in the wilderness
never repay), that no imaginable degree of profusion on
the part of Parliament, profuse as Parliament has of late
years become, could come up to the mark of seriously
entertaining so monstrous a scheme.

MONDAY, DECEMBER 7, 1846

THE RETURNS in our Saturday's paper of the number of
persons receiving relief from the Irish Government in
the form of public employment, and the weekly expense
of that relief, are calculated to inspire serious thoughts
in the most reckless promoter of an extended poor-law
for Ireland.

Three hundred thousand able-bodied Irishmen now
receive wages, and what is called employment, from a
public authority; and the expenditure for the purpose
has nearly reached half a million per month. It is difficult to imagine how under such circumstances it could
be less. Eight months have to elapse before the next
harvest; whatever may be the distress now, it must be-

come greater during all that time, and if the distress did not, the clamour for assistance undoubtedly would. Four millions therefore are the smallest outlay we have still to look forward to, in addition to the whole of what has already been expended. But great as is the present amount, it is a less alarming symptom than the rapidly progressive increase, and even *that* is less formidable than the effects already produced on the minds and conduct of the labouring class. The bitterest enemy of a poor-law with out-door relief could hardly have anticipated so instantaneous and rank a luxuriance of every form of demoralization which could have been expected from the worst permanent poor-law ever proposed. The whole Irish people are rushing with one impulse to fasten themselves upon the taxes. No one will consent to work, except for Government wages. No wonder— they are higher than any other description of wages, and the work well known to be nominal. The small farmers, though they pay no rent, do not even sow their lands. A few days ago we quoted the assertion from a Kerry paper, that the county *en masse* had discontinued agricultural operations. What need that any one should provide food for himself? The Government is to feed everybody.

We should like to know in what manner this initiatory specimen of what is to be expected from the proposed Irish poor-law can be explained away by its promoters. The system now in temporary operation differs in no material feature from what they desire to introduce into the permanent institutions of the country. Whatever difference there may be is to the advantage of the temporary system. They demand a law which shall guarantee wages and out-door employment to all the destitute. The present arrangement only differs from this in holding out, not the certainty, but only the hope of wages and employment. If the mere hope has the effects we now see, what may we not expect from the certainty? There is another difference: the poor-law project would lay the obligation of finding wages and employment upon each *parish* in Ireland; the present arrangements impose the burden upon each *barony*. We know not what inexplicable idea haunts some people, of a wonderful difference in efficacy between these two words; but "parish" will raise a spirit as soon as "barony," and every day's experience is giving additional means of judging what sort of spirit it will be.

The present moment is, without exaggeration, the most critical in the history of England's dealings with Ireland. The whole fruits of centuries of oppression and neglect are coming home to us in a single year. The entire population of the country are coming upon us to be fed. And we are called upon to decide instantaneously whether we will or will not undertake the office. There is no retreating, no putting off. The burden of Irish destitution is now to be borne by us. Ireland can no longer suffer alone. We must take our full share of the evil, or put an end to it. For a few weeks or months longer we have the choice which. Wait a year, and we may have it no longer. Wait a year, and the mind of the Irish population may be so thoroughly pauperised, that to be supported by other people may be the only mode of existence they will consent to. There may [be] a Jacquerie, or another ninety-eight, in defence of the rights of sturdy beggary. It may require a hundred thousand armed men to make the Irish people submit to the common destiny of working in order to live.

Under such a mass of impending evil it is no longer enough not to make the eleemosynary system permanent. That system must be promptly put an end to. We must give over telling the Irish that it is our business to find food for them. We must tell them, now and for ever, that it is *their* business. We must tell them that to find or make employment as an excuse for feeding those who have a head to seek for work and hands to do it, is a thing they are *not* to expect either from the Government, or from the barony, or from the parish. They have a right, not to support at the public cost, but to aid and furtherance in finding support for themselves. They have a right to a repeal of all laws and a reform of all social systems which improperly impede them in finding it, and they have a right to their fair share of the raw material of the earth. They have a right to that part of the earth's surface which is as much theirs as any man's, since no man made it, and no man has ever used or improved it. Millions of acres are lying waste, requiring little more than labour to render them productive, and to avoid giving these acres to the destitute, we are giving them, instead, many millions of pounds sterling. We are paying gold with both hands to destroy such industry, independence, and self-reliance as they already have, and we withhold what would cost us little or nothing, and would be to them the fountain spring of those virtues for all time to come.

We have read with ineffable disgust the statement made by that highly respectable paper, the *Dublin Evening Post,* of its reason for not having yet advocated the location of the peasantry as proprietors on the waste lands. It classes the scheme with that of an extended poor-law, as two things on which it has not declared itself, because it sees almost insuperable difficulties in the way of both. Those of the poor-law we need not recapitulate; those of the waste lands consist in the almost insurmountable aversion which, the *Post* says, it cannot disguise from itself the existence of, as to any project for giving up those lands to a peasant proprietary. We look upon this simple assertion as equivalent to the most bitter of the denunciations of which the Irish landlords complain that they are so often the objects from this side of St. George's Channel. And these dogs in the manger, who will neither use the land nor let others use it, expect sympathy and *money* from England! And one of them at a public meeting dared to invoke the precedent of the twenty millions which the nation cheerfully paid for the freedom of the negro! As much and more would it pay,

and pay gladly, for the freedom and comfort of the worse
than serf, the Irish cottier. But its gifts are not for the
serf's master. It did not pay twenty million to the slave-
owner and leave the slaves no better than they were
before. And we are much mistaken if it will go on long
paying half a million a month without insisting on having full value for the money, in the shape of a permanent
improvement in the industrial and economical system of
Ireland.

ENGLAND
and
IRELAND

John Stuart Mill

[*England and Ireland* is reprinted from the 1868 edition published in London by Longmans, Green, Reader, and Dyer. The copy used for reproduction was supplied by courtesy of the Library, Bryn Mawr College.]

ENGLAND AND IRELAND.

Once at least in every generation the question, "What is to be done with Ireland?" rises again to perplex the councils and trouble the conscience of the British nation. It has now risen more formidable than ever, and with the further aggravation, that it was unexpected. Irish disaffection, assuredly, is a familiar fact; and there have always been those among us who liked to explain it by a special taint or infirmity in the Irish character. But Liberal Englishmen had always attributed it to the multitude of unredressed wrongs. England had for ages, from motives of different degrees of unworthiness, made her yoke heavy upon Ireland. According to a well known computation, the whole land of the island had been confiscated three times over. Part had been taken to enrich powerful Englishmen and their Irish adherents; part to form the endowment of a hostile hierarchy; the rest had been given away to English and Scotch colonists, who held, and were intended to hold it, as a garrison against the Irish. The manufactures of Ireland, except the linen manufacture, which was chiefly carried on by these colonists, were deliberately crushed for the avowed purpose of making more room for those of England. The vast majority

of the native Irish, all who professed the Roman
Catholic religion, were, in violation of the faith
pledged to the Catholic army at Limerick, despoiled
of all their political and most of their civil rights, and
were left in existence only to plough or dig the ground,
and pay rent to their task-masters. A nation which
treats its subjects in this fashion cannot well expect to
be loved by them. It is not necessary to discuss the
circumstances of extenuation which an advocate might
more or less justly urge to excuse these iniquities to
the English conscience. Whatever might be their
value in our own eyes, in those of the Irish they had
not, and could not have, any extenuating virtue.
Short of actual depopulation and desolation, or the
direct personal enslaving of the inhabitants, little was
omitted which could give a people cause to execrate
its conquerors. But these just causes of disloyalty, it
was at last thought, had been removed. The jealousy
of Irish industry and enterprise has long ceased, and
all inequality of commercial advantages between the
two countries has been done away with. The civil
rights of the Catholic population have been restored
to them, and (with one or two trifling exceptions) their
political disabilities have been taken off. The prizes
of professional and of political life, in Ireland, England,
and every British dependency, have been thrown open,
in law and in fact, to Catholic as well as Protestant
Irish. The alien Church indeed remains, but is no
longer supported by a levy from the Catholic tillers of
the soil ; it has become a charge on the rent paid by
them, mostly to Protestant landlords. The confiscations have not been reversed ; but the hand of time
has passed over them : they have reached the stage at

which, in the opinion of reasonable men, the reversal of an injustice is but an injustice the more. The representatives of the Irish Catholics are a power in the House of Commons, sufficient at times to hold the balance of parties. Irish complaints, great and small, are listened to with patience, if not always with respect; and when they admit of a remedy which seems reasonable to English minds, there is no longer any reluctance to apply it. What, then, it is thought even by Liberal Englishmen, has Ireland to resent? What, indeed, remains from which resentment could arise? By dint of believing that disaffection had ceased to be reasonable, they came to think that it had ceased to be possible. All grievances, of a kind to exasperate the ruled against the rulers, had, they thought, disappeared. Nature, too, not in her kinder, but in one of her cruellest moods, had made it her study to relieve the conscience of the English rulers of Ireland. A people of whom, according to the Report of a Royal Commission, two millions and a half were for many weeks of each year in a state of chronic starvation, were a sight which might cause some misgiving in a nation that had absolute power over them. But the Angel of Death had stepped in, and removed that spectre from before our gate. An appalling famine, followed by an unexampled and continuous emigration, had, by thinning the labour market, alleviated that extreme indigence which, by making the people desperate, might embitter them, we thought, even against a mild and just Government. Ireland was now not only well governed, but prosperous and improving. Surely the troubles of the British nation about Ireland were now at an end.

It is upon a people, or at least upon upper and middle classes, basking in this fool's paradise, that Fenianism has burst, like a clap of thunder in a clear sky, unlooked for and unintelligible, and has found them utterly unprepared to meet it and to deal with it. The disaffection which they flattered themselves had been cured, suddenly shows itself more intense, more violent, more unscrupulous, and more universal than ever. The population is divided between those who wish success to Fenianism, and those who, though disapproving its means and perhaps its ends, sympathize in its embittered feelings. Repressed by force in Ireland itself, the rebellion visits us in our own homes, scattering death among those who have given no provocation but that of being English-born. So deadly is the hatred, that it will run all risks merely to do us harm, with little or no prospect of any consequent good to itself. Our rulers are helpless to deal with this new outburst of enmity, because they are unable to see that anything on their part has given cause for it. They are brought face to face with a spirit which will as little tolerate what we think our good government as our bad, and they have not been trained to manage problems of that difficulty. But though their statesmanship is at fault, their conscience is at ease, because the rebellion, they think, is not one of grievance or suffering; it is a rebellion for an idea—the idea of nationality. Alas for the self-complacent ignorance of irresponsible rulers, be they monarchs, classes, or nations! If there is anything sadder than the calamity itself, it is the unmistakeable sincerity and good faith with which numbers of Englishmen confess themselves incapable of comprehending it. They know not that the disaffection which neither has nor needs any other motive than aversion to the rulers, is the climax to a long growth of disaffection arising from causes that might have been removed. What seems to them the causelessness of the Irish repugnance to our rule, is the proof that they have almost let pass the last opportunity they are ever likely to have of setting it right. They have allowed what once was indignation against particular wrongs, to harden into a passionate determination to be no longer ruled on any terms by those to whom they ascribe all their evils. Rebellions are never really unconquerable until they have become rebellions for an idea. Revolt against practical ill-usage may be quelled by concessions ; but wait till all practical grievances have merged in the demand for independence, and there is no knowing that any concession, short of independence, will appease the quarrel.

But what, it will be asked, is the provocation that England is giving to Ireland, now that she has left off crushing her commerce and persecuting her religion ? What harm to Ireland does England intend, or knowingly inflict ? What good, that she knows how to give her, would she not willingly bestow ? Unhappily, her offence is precisely that she does not know ; and is so well contented with not knowing, that Irishmen who are not hostile to her are coming to believe that she will not and cannot learn. Calm men, like the clerical authors of the Limerick declaration, who disapprove of Fenianism and of all that the Fenians are doing, and who have no preference for separation in itself, are expressing a deliberate conviction that the English nation *cannot* see or understand what laws and institutions are necessary for a state of society and civilization like that of Ireland. The English people ought to ask themselves, seriously and without prejudice, what it is that gives sober men this opinion of them ; and endeavour to remove it, or humbly confess that it is true, and fulfil the only duty which remains performable by them on that supposition, that of withdrawing from the attempt.

That this desperate form of disaffection, which does not demand to be better governed, which asks us for no benefit, no redress of grievances, not even any reparation for injuries, but simply to take ourselves off and rid the country of our presence—that this revolt of mere nationality has been so long in coming, proves that it might have been prevented from coming at all. More than a generation has elapsed since we renounced the desire to govern Ireland for the English : if at that epoch we had begun to know how to govern her for herself, the two nations would by this time have been one. But we neither knew, nor knew that we did not know. We had got a set of institutions of our own, which we thought suited us— whose imperfections we were, at any rate, used to : we, or our ruling classes, thought, that there could be no boon to any country equal to that of imparting those institutions to her, and as none of their benefits were any longer withheld from Ireland, Ireland, it seemed, could have nothing more to desire. What was not too bad for us, must be good enough for Ireland, or if not, Ireland or the nature of things was alone in fault.

It is always a most difficult task which a people assumes when it attempts to govern, either in the way of incorporation or as a dependency, another people very unlike itself. But whoever reflects on the constitution of society in these two countries, with any sufficient knowledge of the states of society which exist elsewhere, will be driven, however unwillingly, to the conclusion, that there is probably no other nation of the civilized world, which, if the task of governing Ireland had happened to devolve on it, would not have shown itself more capable of that work than England has hitherto done. The reasons are these: First, there is no other civilized nation which is so conceited of its own institutions, and of all its modes of public action, as England is; and secondly, there is no other civilized nation which is so far apart from Ireland in the character of its history, or so unlike it in the whole constitution of its social economy; and none, therefore, which if it applies to Ireland the modes of thinking and maxims of government which have grown up within itself, is so certain to go wrong.

The first indeed of our disqualifications, our conceit of ourselves, is certainly diminishing. Our governing classes are now quite accustomed to be told that the institutions which they thought must suit all mankind since they suited us, require far greater alteration than they dream of to be fit even for ourselves. When they were told this, they have long been in the habit of answering, that whatever defects these institutions may have in theory, they are suited to the opinions, the feelings, and the historical antecedents of the English people. But mark how little they really mean by this vindication. If suitability to the opinions, feelings, and historical antecedents of those

who live under them is the best recommendation of
institutions, it ought to have been remembered, that
the opinions, feelings, and historical antecedents of
the Irish people are totally different from, and in
many respects contrary to those of the English ; and
that things which in England find their chief justification in their being liked, cannot admit of the same
justification in a country where they are detested.
But the reason which recommends institutions to
their own supporters, and that which is used to stop
the mouths of opponents, are far from being always
one and the same.

Let us take as an example, that one of our institutions which has the most direct connexion with the
worst practical grievances of Ireland ; absolute property in land, the land being engrossed by a comparatively small number of families. I am not going to
discuss this institution, or to express, on the present
occasion, any opinion about its abstract merits. Let
these, if we will, be transcendant—let it be the best
and highest form of agricultural and social economy,
for anything I mean to say to the contrary. But I
do say that this is not self-evident. It is not one of
the truths which shine so brilliantly by their own
light, that they are assented to by every sane man
the moment he understands the words in which they
are conveyed. On the contrary, what present themselves the most obviously at the first aspect of this
institution are the objections to it. That a man
should have absolute control over what his own labour
and skill have created, and even over what he has received by gift or bequest from those who created it,
is recommended by reasons of a very obvious charac-

ter, and does not shock any natural feeling. Move-able property can be produced in indefinite quantity, and he who disposes as he likes of anything which, it can fairly be argued, would not have existed but for him, does no wrong to any one. It is otherwise with regard to land, a thing which no man made, which exists in limited quantity, which was the original in-heritance of all mankind, and which whoever appro-priates, keeps others out of its possession. Such ap-propriation, when there is not enough left for all, is at the first aspect, an usurpation on the rights of other people. And though it is manifestly just that he who sows should be allowed to reap, this justice, which is the true moral foundation of property in land, avails little in favour of proprietors who reap but do not sow, and who assume the right of ejecting those who do. When the general condition of the land of a country is such as this, its title to the sub-mission and attachment of those whom it seems to disinherit, is by no means obvious. It is a state of things which has great need of extrinsic recommenda-tions. It requires to be rooted in the traditions and oldest recollections of the people ; the landed families must be identified with the religion of the country, with its nationality, with its ancient rulers, leaders, defenders, teachers, and other objects of gratitude and veneration, or at least of ungrudging obedience.

These conditions have been found, in some con-siderable measure, or at all events, nothing contrary to them has been found, for many centuries, in Eng-land. All that is most opposite to them has at all times existed in Ireland. The traditions and recollections of native Irish society are wholly the contrary way. Before the Conquest, the Irish people knew nothing of absolute property in land. The land virtually belonged to the entire sept; the chief was little more than the managing member of the association. The feudal idea, which views all rights as emanating from a head landlord, came in with the Conquest, was associated with foreign dominion, and has never to this day been recognised by the moral sentiments of the people. Originally the offspring not of industry but of spoliation, the right has not been allowed to purify itself by protracted possession, but has passed from the original spoliators to others by a series of fresh spoliations, so as to be always connected with the latest and most odious oppressions of foreign invaders. In the moral feelings of the Irish people, the right to hold the land goes, as it did in the beginning, with the right to till it. Since the last confiscations, nearly all the land has been owned from generation to generation with a more absolute ownership than exists in almost any other country (except England), by landlords (mostly foreigners, and nearly all of a foreign religion) who had less to do with tilling it, who had less connexion with it of any useful kind— or indeed of any kind, for a large proportion did not even reside on it—than the landowners of any other known country. There are parts of Europe, such as East Prussia, where the land is chiefly owned in large estates, but where almost every landowner farms his own land. In Ireland, until a recent period, any one who knew the country might almost have counted those who did anything for their estate but consume its produce. The landlords were a mere burthen on the land. The whole rental of the country was wasted in maintaining, often in reckless extravagance, people who were not nearly as useful to the hive as the drones are, and were entitled to less respect. These are the antecedents of Irish history in respect to property in land. Let any Englishman put himself in the position of an Irish peasant, and ask himself whether, if the case were his own, the landed property of the country would have any sacredness to his feelings. Even the Whiteboy and the Rockite, in their outrages against the landlord, fought for, not against, the sacredness of what was property in their eyes; for it is not the right of the rent-receiver, but the right of the cultivator, with which the idea of property is connected in the Irish popular mind.

These facts being notorious, and the feelings engendered by them being, in part at least, perfectly reasonable in the eyes of every civilized people in the world except England, it is a characteristic specimen of the practical good sense by which England is supposed to be distinguished, that she should persist to this hour in forcing upon a people with such feelings, and such antecedents, her own idea of absolute property in land. If those who created English manufactures, commerce, navigation, and dominion, to say nothing of English literature and science, had gone to work in this style— had shown this amount of judgment in the adaptation of means to ends—England would at the present time have been in something like the condition of the Papal territory, or of Spain.

Thus much as to the harmony of certain English institutions with the feelings and prepossessions of the Irish people, which, according to the received doctrine of our historical Conservatives, is the first point to be considered in either retaining old institutions or introducing new. But now, apart from the question of acceptability to Ireland, let us consider whether our own laws and usages, at least in relation to land, are the model we should even desire to follow in governing Ireland; whether the circumstances of the two countries are sufficiently similar, to warrant the belief, that things which may work well, or may not be fatally destructive to prosperity, in England, will be useful or innocuous, even if voluntarily accepted by the people of the neighbouring island.

What are the main features in the social economy of Ireland? First, it is a country wholly agricultural. The entire population, with some not very important exceptions, cultivates the soil, or depends for its subsistence on cultivation. In this respect, if all the countries of Europe except Russia were arranged in a scale, Ireland would be at one extremity of the scale, England and Scotland at the other. In Great Britain, not more than a third of the population subsists by agriculture. In most countries of the Continent a great majority do so, though in no country but Russia so great a majority as in Ireland. Ireland, therefore, in this essential particular, bears more resemblance to almost any other country in Europe than she does to Great Britain.

When the agricultural population are but a fraction of the entire people; when the commercial and manufacturing development of the country leaves a large opening for the children of the agriculturists to seek and find subsistence elsewhere than on the soil; a bad tenure of land, though always mischievous, can in some measure be borne with. But when a people have no means of sustenance but the land, the conditions on which the land can be occupied, and support derived from it, are all in all. Now, under an apparent resemblance, those conditions are radically different in Ireland and in England. In England the land is rented and cultivated by capitalist farmers; in Ireland, except in the grazing districts, principally by manual labourers, or small farmers in nearly the same condition in life. The multitude of other differences which flow from this one difference, it would be too prolix to detail. But (what is still more important), in Ireland, where the well-being of the whole population depends on the terms on which they are permitted to occupy the land, those terms are the very worst in Europe. There are many other countries in which the land is owned principally in large masses, and farmed in great part by manual labourers. But I doubt if there be now any other part of Europe where, as a general rule, these farm-labourers are entirely without a permanent interest in the soil. The serfs certainly were not; they could not be turned out of their holdings. The *métayers* in France, before the Revolution, could; and their wretchedness, accordingly, was the bye-word of Europe. There are still métayers in France, but those of them who have not, as many have, other land of their own in full property, are still the disturbing element of rural society. The departments which returned Socialist deputies to the Assemblies of 1848 and 1849 were chiefly those in which métayerism still lingered. The métayers of Italy are, by a custom, as binding as law, irremovable so long as they fulfil their contract. The Prussian peasants, even before the beneficent enfran-

chising legislation of Stein and Hardenberg, had posi-
tive rights in the soil which they could not be deprived of.   It is only in parts of Belgium that it is
a frequent practice for small farmers to hold from
large proprietors, with no other legal protection than
the stipulations of a short lease : but their truly admirable industry owes its vigour to the fact that small
landed properties are always to be had for money, at
prices which they can hope to save.   They, moreover,
live in the midst of a large and thriving manufacturing
industry,which takes off the hands that might otherwise
compete unduly for the soil.   In Ireland alone the whole
agricultural population can be evicted by the mere
will of the landlord, either at the expiration of a lease,
or, in the far commoner case of their having no lease,
at six months' notice.   In Ireland alone the bulk of a
population dependent wholly on the land, cannot look
forward with confidence to a single year's occupation
of it : while the sole outlet for the dispossessed cultivators, or for those whose competition raises the rents
against the cultivators, is expatriation.   So long as
they remain in the country of their birth, their support must be drawn from a source for the permanence
of which they have no guarantee, and the failure of
which leaves them nothing to depend on but the poor-
house.

In one circumstance alone England and Ireland are
alike : the cultivated area of both countries is owned
in large estates by a small class of great landlords.   In
the opinion of great landlords, and of the admirers of
the state of society which produces them, this is
enough : the interest and the wisdom of the landlords
may be implicitly relied on for making everybody

comfortable. Great landlords can do as they like
with their estates, on this side of St. George's Channel;
English landlords are absolute masters of the conditions on which they will let their land ; and why
should not Irish landlords be so ? But in the first
place, English landlords do not let their land to a
labourer, but to a capitalist farmer, who is able to take
care of his own interest. The capitalist has not to
choose between the possession of a farm and destitution; the labourer has. This element subverts the
whole basis on which the letting of farms, as a business transaction, and the foundation of a national
economy, requires to rest. The capitalist farmer
will beware of offering a rent that will leave him no
profit; the peasant farmer will promise any amount
of rent, whether he can pay it or not. England,
moreover, not being a purely agricultural, but a commercial country, even great landlords learn to look at
the management of estates in a somewhat commercial
spirit, and can see their own advantage (where the
love of political influence does not prevent) in making
it the interest of the tenant to improve the land; or,
if they can afford to do so, will often improve it for
him. An average Irish landlord, instead of improving
his estate, does not even put up the fences and farm-
buildings which everywhere else it is the landlord's
business to provide ; they are left to be erected by
the labourer-tenant for himself, and are such as a
labourer-tenant is able to erect. If a tenant here
and there is able and willing to make them a little
better than ordinary, or to add in any other manner
to the productiveness and value of the farm, there is
nothing to prevent the landlord from waiting till it

is done, and then seizing on the result, or requiring from the tenant additional rent for the use of the fruits of his own labour; and so many landlords even of high rank are not ashamed to do this, that it is evident their compeers do not think it at all disgraceful. It is usual to impute the worst abuses of Irish landlordism to middlemen. Middlemen are rapidly dying out, but there was lately a middleman in the county of Clare, under whose landlordship Irish peasants, by their labour and their scanty means, reclaimed a considerable tract on the sea-coast, and founded thereon the flourishing watering-place of Kilkee. The middleman died, his lease fell in, and the tenants fancied that they should now be still better off; but the head landlord, the Marquis Conyngham, at once put on rents equal to the full value of the improvements (in some instances an increase of 700 per cent), and not content with this, pulled down a considerable portion of the town, reduced its population from 1879 to 950, and drove out the remainder to wander about Ireland, or to England or America, and swell the ranks of the bitter enemies of Great Britain.* Did the interest, any more than the good feelings, of this landlord, prevent him from destroying this remarkable creation of industry, and giving its creators cause bitterly to repent that they had ever made it? What might not be hoped from a people who had the energy and enterprise to create a flourishing town under

---

* The outline of these facts is matter of public notoriety. For details, far more impressive than I have ventured to quote, the reader may refer to the pamphlet of the Rev. Sylvester Malone, "Tenant-Wrong Illustrated in a Nutshell; or, a History of Kilkee in Relation to Landlordism during the last Seven Years."

liability to be robbed? And to what sympathy or consideration are those entitled who avail themselves of a bad law to perpetrate what is morally robbery?

When Irishmen ask to be protected against deeds of this description, they are told that the law they complain of is the same which exists in England. What signifies it that the law is the same, if opinion and the social circumstances of the country are better than the law, and prevent the oppression which the law permits? It is bad that one *can* be robbed in due course of law, but it is greatly worse when one actually is. England, with her capitalist farmers and her powerful public opinion, can afford to leave improper power in the hands of her great landlords—not, indeed, without serious evil to her agricultural population, the state of which is generally felt to be the most peccant part of her social condition; not without evil to all over whom power is exercised through the votes of that population; but yet without hindrance to the attainment, by the nation as a whole, of great wealth and prosperity. Ireland is very differently circumstanced. When, as a general rule, the land of a country is farmed by the very hands that till it, the social economy resulting is intolerable, unless either by law or custom the tenant is protected against arbitrary eviction, or arbitrary increase of rent. Nor is there any country of Western Europe save England (unless Spain be an exception) which, if Ireland had belonged to it, would not before this time have seen and acted on that principle; because there is not one which is not familiar with the principle and its bearings, from ample experience. England alone is without such experience of its own, and knows and cares too little about foreign countries to benefit by theirs.

At a particular moment of the revolutionary war, a French armament, led by the illustrious Hoche, was only prevented by stress of weather from effecting a landing in Ireland. At that moment it was on the cards whether Ireland should not belong to France, or at least be organized as an independent country under French protection. Had this happened, does any one believe that the Irish peasant would not have become even as the French peasant? When the great landowners had fled, as they would have fled, to England, every farm on their estates would have become the property of the occupant, subject to some fixed payment to the State. Ireland would then have been in the condition in which small farming, and tenancy by manual labourers, are consistent with good agriculture and public prosperity. The small holder would have laboured for himself and not for others, and his interest would have coincided with the interest of the country in making every plot of land produce its utmost. What Hoche would have done for the Irish peasant, or its equivalent, has still to be done; and any government which will not do it does not fulfil the rational and moral conditions of a government. There is no necessity that it should be done as Hoche would most likely have done it, without indemnity to the losers. A few years ago it might not have been necessary to do as much as he would have done. The distribution of the waste land in peasant properties might then have sufficed. Perhaps even such small measures as that of securing to tenants a moderate compensation, in money or by length of lease, for improvements actually made, and abolishing the unjust privilege of distraining for rent, might have appeased or postponed disaffection, and given to great-landlordism a fresh term of existence. But such reforms as these, granted at the last moment, would hardly give a week's respite from active disaffection. The Irish are no longer reduced to take anything they can get. They have acquired the sense of being supported by prosperous multitudes of their countrymen on the opposite side of the Atlantic. These it is who will furnish the leaders, the pecuniary resources, the skill, the military discipline, and a great part of the effective force, in any future Irish rebellion: and it is the interest of these auxiliaries to refuse to listen to any form of compromise, since no share of its benefits would be for them, while they would lose the dream of a place in the world's eye as chiefs of an independent republic. With these for leaders, and a people like the Irish, always ready to trust implicitly those whom they think hearty in their cause, no accommodation is henceforth possible which does not give the Irish peasant all that he could gain by a revolution—permanent possession of the land, subject to fixed burthens. Such a change may be revolutionary; but revolutionary measures are the thing now required. It is not necessary that the revolution should be violent, still less that it should be unjust. It may and it ought to respect existing pecuniary interests which have the sanction of law. An equivalent ought to be given for the bare pecuniary value of all mischievous rights which landlords or any others are required to part with. But no mercy ought to be shown to the mischievous rights themselves; no scruples of purely English birth ought to stay our hands from effecting, since it has come to that, a real revolution in the economical and social constitution of Ireland. In the completeness of the revolution will lie its safety. Anything less than complete, unless as a step to completion, will give no help. There has been a time for proposals to effect this change by a gradual process, by encouragement of voluntary arrangements; but the volume of the Sibyl's books which contained them has been burned. If ever, in our time, Ireland is to be a consenting party to her union with England, the changes must be so made that the existing generation of Irish farmers shall at once enter upon their benefits. The rule of Ireland now rightfully belongs to those who, by means consistent with justice, will make the cultivators of the soil of Ireland the owners of it; and the English nation has got to decide whether it will be that just ruler or not.

Englishmen are not always incapable of shaking off insular prejudices, and governing another country according to its wants, and not according to common English habits and notions. It is what they have had to do in India; and those Englishmen who know something of India, are even now those who understand Ireland best. Persons who know both countries, have remarked many points of resemblance between the Irish and the Hindoo character; there certainly are many between the agricultural economy of Ireland and that of India. But, by a fortunate accident, the business of ruling India in the name of England did not rest with the Houses of Parliament or the offices at Westminster; it devolved on men

who passed their lives in India, and made Indian interests their professional occupation. There was also
the advantage, that the task was laid upon England
after nations had begun to have a conscience, and not
while they were sunk in the reckless savagery of the
middle ages. The English rulers, accordingly, reconciled themselves to the idea that their business was
not to sweep away the rights they found established,
or wrench and compress them into the similitude of
something English, but to ascertain what they were;
having ascertained them, to abolish those only
which were absolutely mischievous; otherwise to protect them, and use them as a starting point for further steps in improvement. This work of stripping
off their preconceived English ideas was at first done
clumsily and imperfectly, and at the cost of many
mistakes; but as they honestly meant to do it, they
in time succeeded, and India is now governed, if with
a large share of the ordinary imperfections of rulers,
yet with a full perception and recognition of its differences from England. What has been done for India
has now to be done for Ireland; and as we should
have deserved to be turned out of the one, had we not
proved equal to the need, so shall we to lose the other.

It is not consistent with self-respect, in a nation
any more than in an individual, to wait till it is compelled by uncontrollable circumstances to resign that
which it cannot in conscience hold. Before allowing
its government to involve it in another repetition of
the attempt to maintain English dominion over Ireland by brute force, the English nation ought to com-
mune with its conscience, and solemnly reconsider its
position. If England is unable to learn what has to

be learnt, and unlearn what has to be unlearnt, in
order to make her rule willingly accepted by the Irish
people ; or, to look at the hypothesis on its other side,
if the Irish are incapable of being taught the superiority of English notions about the way in which
they ought to be governed, and obstinately persist in
preferring their own ; if this supposition, whichever
way we choose to turn it, is true, are we the power
which, according to the general fitness of things and
the rules of morality, ought to govern Ireland ? If
so, what are we dreaming of, when we give our sympathy to the Poles, the Italians, the Hungarians, the
Servians, the Greeks, and I know not how many other
oppressed nationalities ? On what principle did we
act when we renounced the government of the Ionian
Islands ?

It is not to fear of consequences, but to a sense of
right, that one would wish to appeal on this most
momentous question. Yet it is not impertinent to say,
that to hold Ireland permanently by the old bad
means is simply impossible. Neither Europe nor
America would now bear the sight of a Poland across
the Irish Channel. Were we to attempt it, and a
rebellion, so provoked, could hold its ground but for
a few weeks, there would be an explosion of indignation all over the civilized world ; on this single occasion Liberals and Catholics would be unanimous ;
Papal volunteers and Garibaldians would fight side
by side against us for the independence of Ireland,
until the many enemies of British prosperity had time
to complicate the situation by a foreign war. Were
we even able to prevent a rebellion, or suppress it the
moment it broke out, the holding down by military

violence of a people in desperation, constantly strug-
gling to break their fetters, is a spectacle which Russia
is still able to give to mankind, because Russia is
almost inaccessible to a foreign enemy; but the attempt
could not long succeed with a country so vulnerable
as England, having territories to defend in every part
of the globe, and half her population dependent on
foreign commerce.   Neither do I believe that the
mass of the British people, those who are not yet
corrupted by power, would permit the attempt.   The
prophets who, judging, I presume, from themselves,
always augur the worst of the moral sentiments of
their countrymen, are already asseverating that,
whether right or wrong, the British people would
rather devastate Ireland from end to end and root
out its inhabitants, than consent to its separation
from England. If we believe them, the people of
England are a kind of bloodhounds, always ready to
break loose and perpetrate Jamaica horrors, unless
they, and their like, are there to temper and restrain
British brutality. This representation does not accord
with my experience.   I believe that these prophecies
proceed from men who seek to make their countrymen
responsible for what they themselves are burning to
commit; and that the rising power in our affairs, the
democracy of Great Britain, is opposed, on principle, to
holding any people in subjection against their will.
The question was put, some six months ago, to one
of the largest and most enthusiastic public meetings
ever assembled in London under one roof—" Do you
think that England has a right to rule over Ireland
if she cannot make the Irish people content with her
rule?" and the shouts of "No!" which burst from

every part of that great assemblage, will not soon be forgotten by those who heard them. An age when delegates of working men meet in European Congresses to concert united action for the interests of labour, is not one in which labourers will cut down labourers at other people's bidding. The time is come when the democracy of one country will join hands with the democracy of another, rather than back their own ruling authorities in putting it down. I shall not believe, until I see it proved, that the English and Scotch people are capable of the folly and wickedness of carrying fire and sword over Ireland in order that their rulers may govern Ireland contrary to the will of the Irish people. That they would put down a partial outbreak, in order to get a fair trial for a system of government beneficent and generally acceptable to the people, I readily believe; nor should I in any way blame them for so doing.

Let it not, however, be supposed that I should regard either an absolute or a qualified separation of the two countries, otherwise than as a dishonour to one, and a serious misfortune to both. It would be a deep disgrace to us, that having the choice of, on the one hand, a peaceful legislative revolution in the laws and rules affecting the relation of the inhabitants to the soil, or on the other, of abandoning a task beyond our skill, and leaving Ireland to rule herself, incapacity for the better of the two courses should drive us to the worse. For that it would be greatly the worse even for Ireland, many Irishmen, even Irish Catholics, are probably still calm enough to perceive, if but good government can be had without it.

The mere geographical situation of the two countries makes them far more fit to exist as one nation than as two. Not only are they more powerful for defence against a foreign enemy combined than separate, but, if separate, they would be a standing menace to one another. Parted at the present time and with their present feelings, the two islands would be, of all countries in Europe, those which would have the most hostile disposition towards one another. Too much bitter feeling still remains between England and the United States, more than eighty years after separation ; and Ireland has suffered from England for many centuries, evils compared with which the greatest grievances of the Americans were, in all but their principle, insignificant. The persevering reciprocation of insults between English and American newspapers and public speakers has, before now, brought those two countries to the verge of a war; would there not be even more of this between countries still nearer neighbours, on the morrow of an unfriendly separation ? In the perpetual state of irritated feeling thus kept up, trifles would become causes of quarrel. Disputes more or less serious, even collisions, would be for ever liable to occur. Ireland, therefore, besides having to defend herself against all other enemies, internal and external, without English help, would feel obliged to keep herself always armed and in readiness to fight England. An Irishman must have a very lofty idea of the resources of his country who thinks that this load upon the Irish taxpayer would be easily borne. A war-tax assessed upon the soil, for want of other taxable material, would be no small set-off against what the peasant would gain even by the entire cessation of rent. The burthen of the necessity of being always prepared for war, was no unimportant part of the motive which made the Northern States of America prefer a war at once to allowing the South to secede from the Union. Yet the necessity would not have weighed so heavily on them as it would on Ireland, because they were both the most powerful half of the American Union and the richest. To England, the necessity of being always in a state of preparation against Ireland would be comparatively a less inconvenience, because she already has to maintain, for defence against foreigners, a force that would in general suffice for both purposes. But Ireland would have to create both a fleet and an army; and, after all that could be done, so oppressive would be her sense of insecurity, that she would probably be driven to compromise her newly acquired independence, and seek the protection of alliances with Continental powers. From that moment she would, in addition to her own wars, be dragged into a participation in theirs. Were she to choose the smaller evil, and remain free from any permanent entanglement, all enemies of Great Britain would not the less confidently look forward to an Irish alliance, and to being allowed to use Ireland as a basis of attack against Great Britain. Ireland would probably become, like Belgium formerly, one of the battle-fields of European war: while she would be in not unreasonable fear lest England should anticipate the danger, by herself occupying Ireland with a military force at every commencement of hostilities. On the part of England, the pacific character which English policy has assumed precludes any probability of aggressive war; but the ejected Irish higher classes (for ejected they could scarcely fail to be) would form an element hostile to

Ireland on this side of the Irish Sea, which would be to the Irish Republic what the *émigrés* at Coblentz were to revolutionary France. In all this I am supposing that Ireland would succeed in establishing a regular and orderly government : but suppose that she failed ? Suppose that she had to pass through an interval of partial anarchy first ? What if there were a civil war between the Protestant and Catholic Irish, or between Ulster and the other provinces ? Is it in human nature that the sympathies of England should not be principally with the English Protestant colony, and would not she either help that side, or be constantly believed to be on the point of helping it ? For generations it is to be feared that the two nations would be either at war, or in a chronic state of precarious and armed peace, each constantly watching a probable enemy so near at hand that in an instant they might be at each other's throat. By this state of their relations it is almost superfluous to say that the poorer of the two countries would suffer most. To England it would be an inconvenience ; to Ireland a public calamity, not only in the way of direct burthen, but by the paralyzing effect of a general feeling of insecurity upon industrial energy and enterprise.

But there is a contingency beyond all this, from the possibility of which we ought not to avert our eyes. Ireland might be invaded and conquered by a great military power. She might become a province of France. This is not the least likely thing to befal her, if her independence of England should be followed by protracted disorders, such as to make peaceably disposed persons welcome an armed pacificator capable of imposing on the conflicting parties a common servitude. How bitter such a result of all their struggles ought to be to patriotic Irishmen, I will not stop to show. But I ask any patriotic Englishman what he would think of such a prospect ; and whether he is disposed to run the risk of it, in order that a few hundred families of the upper classes may continue to possess the land of Ireland, instead of its pecuniary value.

All this evil, it may be thought, could be prevented by agreeing beforehand upon a close alliance and perpetual confederacy between the two nations. But is it likely that the party which had effected a separation in home affairs, would desire or consent to unity in foreign relations ? A confederacy is an agreement to have the same friends and enemies, and can only subsist between peoples who have the same interests and feelings, and who, if they fight at all, would wish to fight on the same side. Great Britain and Ireland, if all community of interest between them were cut off, would generally prefer to be on contrary sides. In any Continental complications, the sympathies of England would be with Liberalism ; while those of Ireland are sure to be on the same side as the Pope—that is, on the side opposed to modern civilization and progress, and to the freedom of all except Catholic populations held in subjection by non-Catholic rulers. Besides, America is the country with which we are at present in most danger of having serious difficulties; and Ireland would be far more likely to confederate with America against us, than with us against America. Some may say that this difference of national feeling, if an obstacle to alliance, is, *à fortiori*, a condemnation of union. But even the most Catholic of

Irishmen may reasonably consider that Irish influence in the British Parliament is a great mitigator of British hostility to things with which Ireland sympathizes ; that a Pro-Catholic element in the House of Commons, which no English Government can venture to despise, helps to prevent the whole power of Great Britain from being in the hands of the Anti-Catholic element still so strong in England and Scotland. If there is any party in Great Britain which would not have cause to regret the separation of Ireland, it is the fanatical Protestant party. It may well be doubted if an independent Ireland could in any way give such effective support to any cause to which Ireland is attached, as by the forbearance and moderation which her presence in British councils imposes upon the power which would be likeliest, in case of conflict, to lead the van of the contrary side.

I see nothing that Ireland could gain by separation which might not be obtained by union, except the satisfaction, which she is thought to prize, of being governed solely by Irishmen—that is, almost always by men with a strong party animosity against some part of her population : unless indeed the stronger party began its career of freedom by driving the whole of the weaker party beyond the seas. In return, Irishmen would be shut out from all positions in Great Britain, except those which can be held by foreigners. There would be no more Irish prime-ministers, Irish commanders-in-chief, Irish generals and admirals in the British army and fleet. Not in Britain only, but in all Britain's dependencies—in India and the Colonies, Irishmen would henceforth be on the footing of strangers. The loss would exceed the gain, not only by calculation, but in feeling. The first man in a small country would often gladly exchange positions with the fourth or fifth in a great one.

But why, it may be asked, cannot Ireland remain united with the British Crown by a mere personal tie, having the management of her own affairs, as Canada has, though a part of the same empire? Or why may not Great Britain and Ireland be joined as Austria and Hungary are, each with its own separate administration and legislature, and an equal voice in the joint concerns of both? I answer: The former of these relations would be to Ireland a derogation, a descent from even her present position. She is now at least a part of the governing country. She has something to say in the general affairs of the empire. Canada is but a dependency, with a provincial government, allowed to make its own laws and impose its taxes, but subject to the veto of the mother-country, and not consulted at all about alliances or wars, in which it is nevertheless compelled to join. A union such as this can only exist as a temporary expedient, between countries which look forward to separation as soon as the weaker is able to stand alone, and which care not much how soon it comes. This mode of union, moreover, is still recent; it has stood no trials; it has not yet been exposed to the greatest trial—that of war. Let war come, by an act of the British Government in which Canada is not represented, and from a motive in which Canada is not concerned, and how long will Canada be content to share the burthens and the dangers? Even in home affairs, Ireland would not relish the position of Canada. The veto of the Crown is virtually that of the British Parliament;

and though it might, as in the case of Canada, be discreetly confined to what were considered imperial questions, the decision what questions were imperial would rest with the country in whose councils Ireland would no longer have a voice. It is very improbable that the veto would stop at things which, in the opinion of the subordinate country, were proper subjects for it. Canada is a great way off, and British rulers can tolerate much in a place from which they are not afraid that the contagion may spread to England. But Ireland is marked out for union with England, if only by this, that nothing important can take place in the one without making its effects felt in the other. If the British Parliament could sufficiently shake off its prejudices to use the veto on Irish legislation rightly, it could shake them off sufficiently to legislate for Ireland rightly, or to allow the Irish, as it already allows the Scotch members, to transact the business of their own country mainly by themselves.

These objections would not apply to an equal union, like that which has recently been agreed upon between Austria and Hungary. In that there is nothing humiliating to the pride of either country. But if the Canadian system has had but a short trial, the dual system of Austria and Hungary has had none. It has existed only a bare twelvemonth. Hungary, it is true, has been much longer attached by a personal bond to the reigning family of Austria, and Hungary had a Constitution, with some of the elements of freedom; but Austria had not. The difficulty of keeping two countries together without uniting them, begins with constitutional liberty. Countries very dissimilar in character, and even with some internal freedom, may be governed as England and Scotland were by the Stuarts, so long as the people have only certain limited rights, and the government of the two countries practically resides in a single will above them both. The difficulty arises when the unforced concurrence of both nations is required for the principal acts of their government. This relation, between Austria and Hungary, never existed till now. If an arrangement so untried and so unexampled be happily permanent—if it resist the chances of incurable difference of opinion on the subjects reserved for joint deliberation, foreign relations, finances, and war—its success will be owing to circumstances almost peculiar to the particular case, and which certainly do not exist between Great Britain and Ireland. In the first place, the two countries are nearly equal in military resources and prowess. They have fairly tried themselves against one another in open war, and know that neither can conquer the other without foreign aid. In the next place, while each is equally formidable to the other, each stands in need of the other for its own safety; neither is sufficient to itself for maintaining its independence against powerful and encroaching neighbours. Lastly, they do not start with hostile feelings in the masses of either country towards the other. Hungary has not the wrongs of centuries to revenge; her direct injuries from Austria never reached the labouring classes, but were confined to portions of society whose conduct is directed more by political interest than by vindictive feeling. The reverse of all this is true between Great Britain and Ireland. The most favourable of all combinations of circumstances for the success and permanence of an equal alliance between independent nations under the same crown, exists between Hungary and Austria, the .least favourable between England and Ireland. Nor let it be said that these reasons against an equal alliance are reasons *à fortiori* against union. The only one of them of which this could be said is the alienation of feeling; and this, if the real grounds of bitterness were removed, the close intercourse and community of interest engendered by union would more and more tend to heal: while the natural tendency of separation, either complete or only partial, would be to estrange the countries from each other more and more. It may be added, that the Hungarian population, which has so nobly achieved its independence, has been trained from of old in the management of the details of its affairs, and has shown, in very trying circumstances, a measure of the qualities which fit a people for self-government, greater than has yet been evinced by Continental nations in many other respects far more advanced. The democracy of Ireland, and those who are likely to be its first leaders, have, at all events, yet to prove their possession of qualities at all similar.

For these reasons it is my conviction that the separation of Ireland from Great Britain would be most undesirable for both, and that the attempt to hold them together by any form of federal union would be unsatisfactory while it lasted, and would end either in reconquest or in complete separation. But in however many respects Ireland might be a loser, she would be a gainer in one. Let separation be ever so complete a failure, one thing it would do: it would convert the peasant farmers into peasant proprietors : and this one thing would be more than an equivalent for all that she would lose. The worst government that would give her this, would be more acceptable, and more deservedly acceptable, to the mass of the Irish people, than the best that withheld it ; if goodness of any kind can be predicated of a Government that refuses the first and greatest benefit that can be conferred on such a country. This benefit, however, she can receive from the Government of the United Kingdom, if those who compose that government can be made to perceive that it is necessary and right. This duty once admitted and acted on, the difficulties of centuries in governing Ireland would disappear.

What the case requires is simply this. We have had commissions, under the authority of Parliament, to commute for an annual payment the burthen of tithe, and the variable obligations of copyholders. What is wanted in Ireland is a commission of a similar kind to examine every farm which is let to a tenant, and commute the present variable for a fixed rent. But this great undertaking must not drag its slow length through generations, like the work of those other commissions. The time is passed for a mere amicable mediation of the State between the landlord and the tenant. There must be compulsory powers, and a strictly judicial inquiry. It must be ascertained in each case, as promptly as is consistent with due investigation, what annual payment would be an equivalent to the landlord for the rent he now receives (provided that rent be not excessive) and for the present value of whatever prospect there may be of an increase, from any other source than the peasant's own exertions. This annual sum should be secured to the landlord, under the guarantee of the

State. He should have the option of receiving it directly from the national treasury, by being inscribed as the owner of Consols sufficient to yield the amount. Those landlords who are the least useful in Ireland, and on the worst terms with their tenantry, would probably accept this opportunity of severing altogether their connexion with the Irish soil. Whether this was the case or not, every farm not farmed by the proprietor would become the permanent holding of the existing tenant, who would pay either to the landlord or to the State the fixed rent which had been decided upon; or less, if the income which it was thought just that the landlord should receive were more than the tenant could reasonably be required to pay. The benefit, to the cultivator, of a permanent property in the soil, does not depend on paying nothing for it, but on the certainty that the payment cannot be increased; and it is not even desirable that, in the first instance, the payment should be less than a fair rent. If the land were let below its value, to this new kind of copyholder, he might be tempted to sublet it at a higher rent, and live on the difference, becoming a parasite supported in idleness on land which would still be farmed at a rackrent. He should therefore pay the full rent which was adjudged to the former proprietor, unless special circumstances made it unjust to require so much.* When such circumstances existed, the State

---

* This same provision meets the objection sometimes made, that the worst farmers at present are those who hold on long leases or in perpetuity. Such farmers would not long stand the test of being held strictly to payment of the full amount of what is now a fair rent. They would soon either change their habits or give place to others.

must lose the difference; or if the Church property, after its resumption by the State, yielded a surplus beyond what is required for the secular education of the people, the remainder could not be better applied to the benefit of Ireland than in this manner.

We are told by many (I am sorry that Lord Stanley is one of them) that in a generation after such a change, the land of Ireland would be overcrowded by the growth of population, would be sublet and subdivided, and things would be as bad as before the famine. Just in the same manner we were told that after a generation or two of peasant proprietorship, the whole rural territory of France would be a pauper warren, and its inhabitants would be engaged in " dividing, by logarithms, infinitesimal inheritances." How have these predictions been fulfilled ? The complaint now is that the population of France scarcely increases at all, and the rural population diminishes. And, in spite of the compulsory division of inheritances by the Code Civil, the reunions of small properties by marriage and inheritance fully balance the subdivisions. The obsolete school of English political economists, whom I may call the Tory school, because they were the friends of entail, primogeniture, high rents, great landed properties, and aristocratic institutions generally, predicted that peasant proprietorships would lead not only to excessive population, but to the wretchedest possible agriculture. What has the fact proved ? I will not refer to the standard work on this subject, Mr. W. T. Thornton's " Plea for Peasant Proprietors," or to Mr. Kay's " Social Condition of the People in England and Europe," or to the multitude of authorities cited in my own Political

Economy, or to the more recent careful and thoughtful researches of M. Emile de Laveleye. I will quote
from M. Léonce de Lavergne, at present the stock
authority of the opponents of small landed properties.
What says M de Lavergne in his latest production,
an article in the *Revue des Deux Mondes* of the 1st of
December last? " As a general rule, the lands held
" in small properties are twice as productive as the
" others, so that if this element were to fail us, our
" agricultural produce would be considerably dimi-
" nished." Those who still believe that small peasant
properties are either detrimental to agriculture or
conducive to overpopulation, are discreditably behind
the state of knowledge on the subject. There is no
condition of landed property which excites such intense exertions for its improvement, as that in which
all that can be added to the produce belongs to him
who produces it. Nor does any condition afford so
strong a motive against overpopulation; because it is
much more obvious how many mouths can be supported by a piece of land, than how many hands can
find employment in the general labour market. The
danger of subletting is equally visionary. In the first
place, subletting might be prohibited; but on the
plan I propose there is no necessity for prohibiting it.
If the holder, by his labour or outlay, adds to the
value of the farm, he is well entitled to sublet it if he
pleases. If its value augments from any other cause
than his exertions, it will generally be from the increased prosperity of the country, which will be a
proof that the new system is successful, and that he
may sublet without inconvenience. Only one precau-
tion is necessary. For years, perhaps for generations,

he should not be allowed to let the land by competition, or for a variable rent. His lessee must acquire it as he himself did, on a permanent tenure, at an unchangeable rent, fixed by public authority; that the substituted, like the original, holder may have the full interest of a proprietor in making the most of the soil.

All prognostics of failure drawn from the state of things preceding the famine are simply futile. The farmer, previous to the famine, was not proprietor of his bit of land; he was a cottier, at a nominal rent, puffed up by competition to a height far above what could, even under the most favourable circumstances, be paid, and the effect of which was that whether he gained much or little, beyond the daily potatoes of which his family could not be deprived, all was swept off for arrears of rent. Alone of all working people, the Irish cottier neither gained anything by industry and frugality, nor lost anything by idleness and reckless multiplication. That because he was not industrious and frugal without a motive, he will not be industrious and frugal when he has the strongest motive, is not a very plausible excuse for refusing him the chance. There is also another great change in his circumstances since the famine : the bridge to America has been built. If a population should grow up on the small estates more numerous than their produce can comfortably support, what is to prevent that surplus population from going the way of the millions who have already found in another continent the field for their labour which was not open to them at home? And the new emigrants, there would then be reason to hope, would not, as now, depart in bitterness, nor return in enmity.

The difficulty of governing Ireland lies entirely in our own minds; it is an incapability of understanding. When able to understand what justice requires, liberal Englishmen do not refuse to do it. They understood the injustice of the political disabilities of Catholics, and they removed them. They understand the injustice of endowing an alien Church, and they have made up their minds that the endowment shall no longer continue. Foreign nations and posterity will judge England's capacity for government, by the ability she now shows to overcome the difficulty of seeing what justice requires in the matter of Irish landed tenure. To her it is a difficulty. Other nations see no difficulty in it. To the Prussian Conservative, Von Raumer, and the French Liberal, Gustave de Beaumont, it was already, thirty years ago, the most obvious thing in the world. It will seem so to future generations. Posterity will hardly be just to the men of our time. The superstitions of landlordism once cast off, it will be difficult to imagine what real and deep-rooted superstitions they once were, and how much of the best moral and even intellectual attributes was compatible with them. But not the less is he in whom any principle or feeling has become a superstition, convulsively clung to where the reasons fail, unfit to have the power of imposing his superstition on people who do not share it. If we cannot distinguish the essentials from the accidents of landed property; if it is and must remain to us the Ark of the Covenant, which must be neither touched nor looked into, for however indispensable a need, it is our duty to retire from a country where a modification of the constitution of landed property is the primary necessity of social life. It may be that there is not wisdom or courage in English statesmen to look the idol in the face. We may be put off with some insignificant attempt to give tenants the hope of compensation for " unexhausted improvements"—something which, ten years, or even two years ago, would have been valuable as a pledge of good will, a sign of just purposes, and a ground of hope that more would be done when experience had proved this to be insufficient; but which would not even then have been accepted as payment in full, and is now scarcely worth offering as an instalment. Even this, if proposed, ought to be voted for in preference to nothing. If a debtor acknowledges only sixpence when he owes a pound, he should be allowed to pay that sixpence; but let us not for a moment intermit the demand, that the remaining balance be paid up before the otherwise inevitable hour of bankruptcy arrives.

For let no one suppose that while this question remains as it is, the sum of all other things that could be done for Ireland would at all alleviate our difficulties there. Abundance of other things, indeed, require to be done. There are not only the religious endowments to be resumed, but their proceeds have to be applied, in the most effectual way possible, to the promotion of Irish improvement. The Church lands and tithes, augmented by the Maynooth endowment and the *regium donum*, would be more than enough, with the sums already appropriated to the purpose, to afford a complete unsectarian education to the entire people, including primary schools, middle schools, high schools, and universities, each grade to be open free of cost to the pupils who had most distinguished themselves in the grade below it. The administration of local justice, of local finance, and other local affairs, requires the hand of the reformer even more urgently than in England. Such minor matters as, though of small account in themselves, would help to conciliate Irish feeling, ought not to be neglected. Those are not wrong who have urged that, with parity of qualifications, Irishmen (when not partisans) should have the preference for Irish appointments ; and there is no good reason why the heir to the throne should not, during part of every year, reside and hold a Court at Dublin. Those purely material improvements to which voluntary enterprise is not adequate, should, with due consideration and proper precautions, receive help from the State. The possible consolidation of Irish railways under State management, or under a single company by concession from the State, is already engaging the attention of our public men ; and advances for drainage, and other improvements on a large scale, are, in a country so poor and backward as Ireland, economically admissible : only not on the plan hitherto adopted, of lending to the landlords, that the entire benefit of the improvement may accrue to their rents. It is scarcely credible that a large extension of *such* advances has within the last few weeks been publicly propounded as a remedy for Fenianism and all other Irish ills, and that a bill for that purpose, promoted by the Government, is actually before Parliament. We have heard of people who would have cried fire during the Deluge : these people, if they had lived at the time of the Deluge, would have proposed to stop it by turning on a little more water.

But none of these things—not even the cashiering

of the Irish Protestant Church—nor all these things taken together, could avail to stop the progress of Irish disaffection, because not one of them comes near its real cause. Matters of affronted feeling, and of minor or distant pecuniary interest, will occupy men's minds when the primary interests of subsistence and security have been cared for, and not before. Let our statesmen be assured that now, when the long deferred day of Fenianism has come, nothing which is not accepted by the Irish tenantry as a permanent solution of the land difficulty, will prevent Fenianism, or something equivalent to it, from being the standing torment of the English Government and people. If without removing this difficulty, we attempt to hold Ireland by force, it will be at the expense of all the character we possess as lovers and maintainers of free government, or respecters of any rights except our own; it will most dangerously aggravate all our chances of misunderstandings with any of the great powers of the world, culminating in war; we shall be in a state of open revolt against the universal conscience of Europe and Christendom, and more and more against our own. And we shall in the end be shamed, or, if not shamed, coerced, into releasing Ireland from the connexion; or we shall avert the necessity only by conceding with the worst grace, and when it will not prevent some generations of ill blood, that which if done at present may still be in time permanently to reconcile the two countries.

THE END.

1 2 3 4 5 6 7 8 9 10 11 12 13   88 87 86 85 84 83 82 81 80 79

DATE DUE

Henning — 2-16-82			